WORLDS TO CONQUER: STEVE REEVES

EXTRAORDINARY PRAISE FOR CHRIS LeCLAIRE AND
WORLDS TO CONQUER

"A must read authorized biography entitled *Worlds To Conquer*...The author's text is the product of meticulous research that reveals all facets of Reeves' life, augmented by colorful interviews, providing a who's who in the iron game."

- *FLEX* Magazine

"There is plenty to learn in this new biography, even for the most die-hard Reeves fans...for bodybuilding history buffs, and Steve Reeves fans this book is a great learning tool."

- *IRONMAN* Magazine

"This book *Worlds To Conquer* is historically important, both as a social document as well as a fortuitous tribute to one of the greatest physical culturist the world as ever known."

- *HEALTH & STRENGTH* Magazine

"LeClaire's book *Worlds To Conquer* helps you to know the real Steve Reeves. If you read this book you are going to separate the fact from the fiction and will have a true insight into him.

- *JACK LALANNE*, Global Fitness Legend

"*WORLDS TO* CONQUER is not a how to book on training, it is more of an exploration of Steve Reeves life. Upon finishing this book, you will have a feel for the very private man that Reeves always was."

- *MUSCLE & FITNESS* Magazine

"*Worlds To Conquer* must sit on the library shelf of anyone purporting knowledge of bodybuilding during the reign of Steve Reeves."

- *FLEX* Magazine

Genevieve Grad with Steve Reeves in 1963 *Sandokan The Great*. Courtesy Steve Reeves

STEVE REEVES

WORLDS TO CONQUER

The Authorized Biography

By

Christopher D. LeClaire

USN Dive Locker Press * Massachusetts

Copyright 2017 by Christopher LeClaire

All rights reserved. No part of this book may be reproduced in any manner whatsoever without written permission from the author, except in the case of brief quotations embodied in critical articles or reviews.

For information address: Christopher LeClaire, USN Dive Locker Press, P.O. Box 116, South Chatham, MA. 02659 USA

Second Edition ISBN 978-0-9676754-0-4

A first edition of this book was published in 1999 by Monomoy Press. It is reprinted here by USN Dive Locker Press.

OPM 9 8 7 6 5 4 3 2 1

Book and Cover Design by Christopher LeClaire

Dedicated to my parents,

Col. Hillary & Anne LeClaire

A 1954 publicity photo for MGM *Athena* starring Jane Powell, Steve Reeves and Debbie Reynolds.

CONTENTS

Introduction

Chapter 1	The Early Years, Home on The Range	15
Chapter 2	Oakland	34
Chapter 3	South Pacific	62
Chapter 4	The Iron Game	70
Chapter 5	Drive, Desire & Discipline	84
Chapter 6	Mr. America	100
Chapter 7	New York	112
Chapter 8	Muscle Beach	126
Chapter 9	Still Striving For First	138
Chapter 10	London	162
Chapter 11	Experiments	178
Chapter 12	Hercules	200
Chapter 13	Unchained & Running	218
Chapter 14	Cowboy Redux	254
Chapter 15	Sunset	266
Chapter 16	Last Call	270

Chronology & Acknowledgements   *275*

Reeves posing for a publicity shot during *Hercules*, 1957. Courtesy Milton T. Moore, Jr.

INTRODUCTION

May 9th, 1993, Mid-flight from Boston to San Diego. I am en route to meet Steve Reeves. As the plane crosses the continent, I try to imagine how he must look at 67. The only photos I have seen of him were taken more than thirty years ago, in the prime of his bodybuilding days and early in his movie career. I take a folder out of my briefcase and study a picture. Reeves on a beach, in costume for Hercules, full beard, toga, thighs flexed, massive arms outstretched, as if in greeting, as if to embrace the world. I can't superimpose the image of an older Reeves over this photo, can't add a layer of age to depict what he looks like now.

Reeves has granted the interview only after months of requests. When I first called him in February of 1993 to approach him with the proposal for a book about his life and movie career he had responded with a flat, *"I don't find my career all that interesting, thank you anyways."* During the conversation, I broached the subject of an interview at least three times, but he put me off, finally deflecting my idea by suggesting that I get back to him in three weeks. Exactly three weeks later I called and once more Reeves was reluctant to agree to an interview. This time, however, the call lasted longer. Again, I was struck by the deep timbre of his voice, remembering rumors I'd heard about his movies being dubbed because his voice was high pitched. We talked about Sergio Leone and Edward D. Wood along with other preeminent directors he had worked with. As we continued to talk, he suddenly expressed resentment that people thought about him only as the role of Hercules. *"That's the problem,"* Steve said. *"Out of the seventeen films I starred in, only two were Hercules movies. People think I did ten."* We went on to talk about his days as a champion bodybuilder and his life now. He informed me of the recent passing of his wife, Aline, a marriage of 26 years and the toll it had been taking on his life. And lastly, his ranch in the hills outside Escondido, along with his prized Morgan horses. Before we hang up, he conceded to an interview. *"Okay,"* he said reluctantly. *"I suppose I can give you one hour. One hour."* For this I am flying across the country. To relieve a bout of nerves, I flip through my notes. As I review the questions I intend to ask, I turn pass another 8X10 photo, the same image that initially motivated me to write his life story. In the summer of 1991, while thumbing through a newsstand issue of *IronMan* Magazine, a photo of George Eiferman caught my attention. Taken in 1956, the shot was of Eiferman, a former Mr. America, posing on a California beach with another bodybuilder. Comparing the two bodybuilders, I asked myself which physique I would choose and be inspired by for my own training. Eiferman had the mass and weight of a big competitor, but it was the other athlete who had in addition to muscle and brawn, outstanding proportion and an arresting grace. The caption read: *"George Eiferman with one-time training partner and roommate Steve Reeves, 'MR. EVERYTHING.'"* Although the name was somewhat unfamiliar to me, I could not dismiss the fact that I had seen Reeves before.

    I began searching through used book stores in Boston, buying up old muscle magazines wherever I could find them, looking for stories and photos of Reeves. I soon learned that he was an internationally known bodybuilding champion and in the late 1940's had won the Mr. America (1947) contest - the youngest ever to do so - an accomplishment he soon topped by winning the Mr. World (1948) and Mr. Universe (1950) titles as well. One day, a college professor of mine saw a photo of Reeves in a file on my desk and said, *"I remember him. When I was a kid in the 1950's, I used to go to all the movies houses to see him. He was Hercules!"* I understood then why that first photo in *IronMan* had seemed so familiar. As a ten-year old, I would sit transfixed in front of the television on Saturday mornings watching old movies. *Morgan*

The Pirate. Hercules. The Thief of Baghdad. The genre was known as 'Sword & Sandal' classics, and identifying with the heroes of these mythological tales, I could not get enough of them. So, Steve Reeves the world champion bodybuilder, was the same Reeves whose cinematic exploits I had marveled at as a kid. Rather than satisfying my curiosity, this information only heightened it. I went in search of a book about Reeves life and career that would tell me more about him but had no luck. At this time in 1991, there was not even a fan club established and dedicated to Steve Reeves, although two were to be created in the mid-1990s, one in Naro, Italy and the other in California. The more difficult it was to find information, the more driven I became to learn more. I searched for back issues of *Muscular Development, Your Physique,* and even *Strength & Health* going as far back as the forties. The items I uncovered only added to his mystique: Reeves, known as the man with the perfect physique was reclusive and very private. While acting in films produced by famed Joseph E. Levine he met and married a princess and became a count. He had lived in Switzerland for ten years, had spent time as a rodeo rider. He had appeared on Broadway and in night club acts. Later, I was to learn that many of these 'facts' were not true and I faced the difficulty of separating truth from here say. One *Health & Strength* article said that he was 6'4" while others wrote that he was 5'7" and directors had to get shorter actors to play opposite him. Another article wrote that his films were dubbed because his voice was high pitched. I read that he had a Brooklyn accent and that he had no voice at all due to heavy steroid use. I read he had joined the Mae West traveling road show and that he had performed his own stunts in many of his films. And most of all that Steve portrayed *Superman* in the 1950s television series.

Which of these rumors were fact? Who was this man? What drove him to develop such an ideal physique? What made him tick? What was it like to be an idol for millions? Why, after rising to the heights in two fields had he dropped from the public arena so suddenly? What had become of him? Where was he now?

I spent the next year and half (1991-1993) looking for answers. At first, I envisioned a book that would celebrate Reeves as both a bodybuilder and actor, but soon I saw a larger purpose. His story was a remarkably inspiring one offering a reader many lessons from a life well led.

At the motel Reeves has recommended as inexpensive and safe I try to nap but am unable to lie down for more than ten minutes. At this time in my life, I was twenty-three years old just completing a tour of duty as a US Navy DIVER and currently enrolled full-time in college. So, meeting Steve Reeves and writing his life story was my next big goal to achieve. As arranged, I call Reeves that afternoon to let him know I was now in town and to reconfirm our appointment the following morning. Again, he makes a point of saying he can only give me one hour of his time. The next day, it takes me no more than fifteen minutes to reach Reeves' horse ranch. As I drive up the winding dirt road, I check my watch repeatedly, taken by the sense that it is important that I am on time. It is exactly 9 a.m. when I spot the fence post to which is attached a mailbox, ordinary except for the name - REEVES. As I drive into the circular driveway bordered by orange groves, I see two figures in a field maneuvering a long irrigation pipe - a makeshift watering system I am soon to learn. One is a woman, the other a man. Reeves' hair is windblown. He is dressed in sweat pants and a long shirt. The distance of yards and of years makes no difference. I know it is Reeves. I yell out a greeting. He waves and calls back that he'll be there in a minute. As he approaches, I sense his trusting smile. We greet one another and shake hands with his Rottweiler at his side. Steve's hair is gray, his face older, but his eyes are still young, Hollywood blue. Reeves leads me into the main house and shows me to the den, while he goes to change from his work clothes. My attention immediately goes to the top shelf of a bookcase where Reeves first-place, bronze 1950 Mr. Universe trophy of Eugene Sandow, the legendary father of bodybuilding sits. I recall seeing a photo of Reeves holding the trophy in his arms of victory at the conclusion of the contest in London, the year

Steve was only twenty- four.

    Soon Reeves returns. Zorro the Rottweiler joins us easing some of the tension in the air, and I have to smile this is exactly the dog central casting would have chosen for Steve Reeves. I notice Reeves forearms and biceps still reveal a once Mr. Universe with well-defined muscles and definition still apparent. He carries himself like a star. We sit down in the living room at opposite facing arm chairs ready to discuss my proposed biography about his life. The room is comfortable and airy. The windows look's out onto a garden courtyard where huge poplar trees sway from the Anza desert winds. After a minute or two of small talk aware that my promised one hour is slipping by, I hand over the proposal I have in mind. As Reeves scans the sample chapters and proposed photos I have put together, I wonder what is going through his mind. At last he takes off his reading glasses. There is a hint of hesitation. *"It's good work Chris,"* he says, *"but it's only a skeleton of my life."*

    That day we begin. We delve back the skeleton of Reeves' remarkable life and career and working together begin to relive his inspiring life and career, setting the record straight. Over the next seven years, including two summer-breaks from college when I lived and worked for Reeves at his California Morgan horse ranch, I assisted with both property maintenance, as well as and the care of his prized Morgan horses, alongside his girlfriend Deborah and her two children. At this point onward, I undertake a unique journey of discovery that leads me throughout the state of California, Montana, New York and Montreal, and eventually to an appreciation and understanding of the character of Steve Reeves.

I hope you enjoy it.

Christopher LeClaire

Chatham, Massachusetts, December 2017

Author Christopher LeClaire with Steve Reeves in the Valley Center, 1993.
Photo by Deborah Englehorn

Immense and immortal was the strength of Hercules, like the world and the Gods to whom he belonged. Yet from lesser man he learned one eternal truth - that even the greatest carries within it a measure of mortal weakness.

Hercules Titanus Films, 1957

A Hollywood portfolio image taken of Steve in 1952. Courtesy Steve Reeves

CHAPTER ONE

The Early Years, Home on The Range

"I often wonder how it would have been if my father hadn't died. I probably would have never left Montana and would have grown up to be a rancher just like him. Then things would have been so much quieter, and life would have been much more tranquil."

-Steve Reeves road trip, Pine Valley, CA June 1994

"Montana is my real home," Reeves told me one night while we were eating dinner. *"It's the place where I was born and raised and is undoubtedly the place I will return to. I have this inner connection with the place, something that is indescribable, but real. I definitely want to be buried up there, somewhere deep in the mountains of Montana."*

Spend any time with him and it soon becomes clear that no matter where he has lived or worked his home state has always maintained a fierce pull on Steve Reeves. To arrive at even an elementary understanding of the man, his emotional geography, his profound appreciation for nature, his rugged independence it is necessary to go back to the beginning, to Montana.

Peerless, Montana is located in Daniels County and is sixteen miles south of Saskatchewan, Canada, eighty-three miles west of the North Dakota border. Before 1900 there were no permanent settlements in the region and the territory was known mostly for its outlaws. Eventually it would become cowboy country, but long before that it was peopled by the Assiniboin and Lakota. In the early 1800's the Lewis & Clark expedition traveled through the area. Then in 1829, when the American Fur Company established a trading post at Fort Union about eighty-five miles to the southeast, trappers began working the plains.

The nearest town of importance is Scobey, located on the banks of the Poplar River, and by 1924 it was the single largest wheat loading center in America. The rich grasslands were converted to fields by single-bottom horse drawn plows and hired 'gang plows' pulled by steam engines. Today the town has a city park, a municipal pool, five churches, one school and an airport with a four-thousand-foot runway. The County courthouse, a wood frame building once a brothel, stands in the northwest comer. Built to serve a farm community, Scobey remains essentially a one street town where single story buildings have two-story fronts, like those of frontier towns in the old western movies.

Throughout Scobey, Richland, and Peerless fields of wheat still stretch beyond view, dominating the landscape, undulating like the waves of some vast inland ocean.

The horizons are limitless, unbroken even by trees. The native growth is bunch grass, sagebrush and buffalo grass and reaches no taller than a man's thigh. The country possesses a beauty that edges into the soul, and yet it is a severe land, a land that tests a person's strength.

Steve Reeves was born here. His ancestors were men of the northwest, a mythical breed around whom the epic of the American West was woven: Rodeo performers, mule skinners, gold miners, trail riders and ranchers.

His father, Lester Dell Reeves, was born in Windom, Minnesota in 1899, the son of Sylvester Reeves and Jessie Day Reeves. In family history handed down through three generations, Sylvester Reeves remains a mystery. Little is known about him except that he was a real ladies' man, and it was this flaw that led to his divorce from Jessie.

In 1916, Jessie moved to Richland, Montana with her second husband Jack Peters and her three sons by Sylvester, Lester, Ted, and Claude. A fourth son, seventeen-year old Archie, stayed briefly in Minnesota with his father. A year later, he joined his mother and soon after died of pneumonia.

When Jessie and Jack Peters filed papers for their homestead in 1915, the area had just been surveyed and homesteaders were joining squatters. Many of the settlers emigrating during this time had few material possessions and often little knowledge of farming. Only fifteen percent survived the first year. Those who stayed were either the stubborn ones who just wouldn't quit, or people who had nothing and nowhere to go back to. Jessie belonged to both camps. For a while, she worked in Burton's Restaurant in Scobey and later she, Jack and her son Lester leased land for a ranch on the Sandy Bench area, nine miles north of Richland. Jesse did a man's work on the ranch and loved to ride horses. She was a strong woman, clearly comfortable outdoors.

Jesse Reeves, Steve's grandmother stands beside her work horse and ranch dog, 1925. Courtesy Claire Boyce

A family photograph of Lester Reeves at twenty-four reveals strong Welsh bones, dark hair, and lantern jawed good looks, looks a camera loves. In it is the image of the man his only son would grow to be. Even today, townspeople in Scobey remark on the striking similarities between Steve and his father Lester. *"Steve is taller than Les,"* remembers Richland native Rodman Miller. *"But he's there all right, old Lester. You can see it in Stevie's eyes."* And in his strength. Even in Montana where a man was judged by his brawn, Lester's strength was legendary. Today, nearly seventy years after his death older Scobey residents still speak about him with the awe reserved for heroes. They tell of how he would take an object like a pot-bellied stove, heavy enough to require three or four men and move it by himself *"Ol'Les was a stocky fella, around six feet, 200 pounds easy, real strong,"* remembers Miller who was a young boy when his father teamed with Lester. *"Everybody liked him. Les was such a bear, such a strong man."* Miller recalls once when his father and Lester were rigging up a team of three (six horses, in rows of two) a big gray team, tall and rangy. *"They were having problems with the horses as they were acting real skittish,"* Miller remembers *"So Lester said, 'hold on here Frank, I got an idea.' He went around behind the horses, grabbed both tails, and jumped up onto the horse's hind quarters yelling out 'go ahead, Frank. try'em now!' But before my father could finish, ol'Les went flying off, bucked clear across the barnyard! Well ol' Les just got up and walked back to the horses, laughing, like nothing in the world could hurt or scare him. He just loved the outdoors. And he'd never tire. He'd work some 12, 16 hours a day."* Miller pauses here, as if he has not yet conveyed the true portrayal of Lester Reeves. *"And his strength,"* he says again. *"I'll tell you! Damn he was strong!!*

When Lester finished high school he primarily farmed with his partner Frank, and also worked as a contractor, digging cellars, building barns and sometimes houses. For autumn, the pair harvested wheat. If he had any dreams, any longings, any stirring of wanderlust or imaginings of a life outside the county lines that he confided to Frank Miller during the long hours the two, worked side by side, they remain long forgotten.

Remembrances such as Rodman Miller's memories are the only things Steve have to create a sense of a father he would never know.

If it were possible Steve would ask his father many things. *"I would ask him about the choices he made in life,"* he says.

"Why he did what he did, and if he could do things differently, how would he do them over again."

Perhaps his mother Golden knew answers to questions like these, but they were never things she discussed with her son Steve.

Golden Viola Boyce was the daughter of a neighboring rancher. According to her brother Claire she was always happy, cheerful and as sunny as her name suggested.

The Boyce's were English and Irish. Steve's maternal grandfather, Steven Boyce, was born in Mansfield, Ohio in 1857. He crossed the plains to California, homesteaded in Washington state and drifted a bit, working as a gold miner, mule skinner, logger, and eventually, cowboy.

In 1879, he drove a herd of cattle from Oregon to Montana and when the rest of the crew returned west he stayed on, one of the hundreds of other homesteaders who located in Daniels County, lured by the promise of 360-acre homesteads.

The fertile land attracted Steven Boyce and caused the drifter in him to finally put down roots. On November 3, 1890 Boyce married the sweet-faced Edith Henderson, a Canadian by birth who had grown up in Peoples Creek, Montana. He was thirty-two, she was sixteen.

The couple moved to Warrick, Montana, built their homestead and began raising children. Seven of their nine reached adulthood. Hardworking, honest, an idealist, Boyce was dogged by misfortune. His determination and the devastation's in his life are detailed in *It's Hard To Kill A Cowboy,* a family history written by his son and granddaughter, Claire and Sharron Boyce.

Stephen and Edith Boyce in 1890. Courtesy Claire Boyce

His investment in the Palace Hotel in Havre was wiped out by a fire in 1918. He moved to a new home in Peerless, thirty miles west of Scobey, and his horse ranch was successful until all the horses in the county locoed and had to be destroyed. A head of cattle unfortunately died off by hoof and mouth disease. His sheep herd were wiped out by the thirties drought. *"In his lifetime, Dad saw plenty of tragedy,"* Claire Boyce wrote.

By the time Steven Boyce's daughter Golden turned eighteen and fell in love with Lester Reeves Goldie, definitely knew the face and name of hard times.

That year Julia Fouhy and Goldie were inseparable. Local Scobey resident Lavina Powell, Julia's younger sister recalls watching the two laugh and dance together. *"Goldie was real beautiful back then. She and my sister used to go together to the Quadrilles,* (square dances on horseback which were a popular event in Scobey at the time)." She remembers her envy for Goldie when she started dating Lester. *"Lester was friendly, very physically built, like a boxer or weight lifter. Well, he and Goldie were simply the most lovey, doviest. It used to make me sick to my stomach watching them kissing and hug,"* Laughs Powell.

Following a brief courtship, the couple were married in the Scobey Methodist Church on April 3, 1924. That summer, they moved northwest of Richland, to a small, two-room house built on the land Lester had purchased with his mother and stepfather.

"Unfortunately, Golden really changed after the marriage," her brother Claire recalls. *"She was always a jolly person, but shortly after the marriage, she got pretty hard about things. Lester, on the other hand, was always laughing, very jolly. When alone, individually they were all right, but when you put the two of them together, matters got mighty hot."*

Steve recalls, *"My mother used to tell me that when she and my father would get in an argument and could not resolve the situation, she would say, 'Lester I'm going home to mother. I can't deal with this.' She would go and stay with my grandparents for a few days, and then when things would calm down, she would return to my father."*

In December 1925, a year and a half after the wedding, Goldie left Lester, once and for all. Eight months pregnant at the time, Golden moved to Glasgow where her brother Steve and wife lived for both family support, and to be near the best hospital in North Eastern Montana.

There in Glasgow, Montana on January 21st, 1926, Stephen Lester Reeves was born. A few days later, Golden and her infant son moved to her parents' ranch in Peerless, Montana.

Lester Dell Reeves and wife Golden Boyce Reeves, 1926. Courtesy Steve Reeves

Steve at age six months old, 1926. Courtesy Steve Reeves

The separation was difficult on everyone. In the months following Goldie's departure, Lester rarely saw his son Steve, although occasionally hearing of news about the two of them. Through friends he learned about Goldie's trip to visit relatives in outside Glasgow that summer, and of his son's first contest. At six months old, Steve had taken first place in The Healthiest Baby Contest at the county fair.

Meanwhile, Lester spent most of his time working in the wheat fields and putting together threshing teams for the fall season. Still, sadness at the loss of his wife and only son was apparent.

"It was early fall of 1927 when I remember riding alongside Lester," recalls Rodman Miller, a Scobey native who knew Steve when he was a young boy. *"I guess I reminded Les of his son that was not around, so he had me ride along with him, sitting beside him, telling stories. I guess it helped his loneliness."*

One day that autumn, Lester gave Rodman a gift, two silver quarters. *"Here,"* Les said. *"Here's fifty cents for you and your brother to split. Be a good boy and I'll see you in a couple of weeks."* The next day, Lester and Frank brought their harvested wheat to McCabe's Grain Mills in Richland. That was the last time Frank Miller ever saw his partner Lester.

Following the sale, Lester made arrangements to meet with another crew in Coalridge, some six miles west of the North Dakota border. Work went smoothly that morning with no premonition of disaster. It was nearly noon when Beach Beachler heard one of the other men swearing out loud. He saw the crew member attempting to free a pitchfork jammed in the gears of the threshing machine, and then saw Lester quickly moving in to help. Beach then heard a sharp crack of breaking metal, and then watched in horror as a prong broke off the pitchfork and shot into Lester's belly, dropping him to his knees.

Lester managed to pull the 10-inch prong from his stomach, but, needed the help of the other men to make it to a nearby truck. The men wrapped Lester in blankets, placed him in the back of the pick-up and headed for St. Joseph's Hospital in nearby Minot, North Dakota. The doctor operated, but Lester's spleen had been punctured, and thus experienced massive bleeding. The following morning, Lester was brought back to Scobey in hopes of a slow recovery, but that afternoon, on October 17, 1927 Lester Dell Reeves passed away. He was only twenty-eight years old.

The funeral for the popular farmer was held in the same Methodist Church where months earlier he and Goldie wed.

Following the service, Lester was buried in the local Scobey Cemetery. Today his simple headstone engraved with his name, the years of his birth and death lies nearly hidden in the rear of the burying grounds.

"I was thinking about my father today," Reeves said recently. *"He got killed at twenty-eight. If I had died at twenty-eight, I would not have had a movie career."*

The death of his father was a pivotal loss in his life, creating an emptiness never filled, questions never answered. The memory of Lester's death retold to Steve by Richland natives, has taken on the power of myth, details that still haunt. Even today, a ranch hand's carelessness with a pitchfork will cause Reeves to explode with anger.

After Lester's death, Steven Boyce became even more of a father figure to his young grandson. Boyce gave Steve his first horse, a docile creature named Old Dan, and by the time the boy was three, had taught him to ride. By the time Steve was six, he was an accomplished horseman, herding sheep for Boyce as easily as the most seasoned ranch hand. Many years later, fellow actors would be amazed by Steve's equestrian skills, and movie stunt coordinators would seek his advice when planning action scenes.

In spite of his father's death, the memory that emerges of this time is of a relatively happy childhood. Remembering these years Reeves talks with joy about Old Dan, the stilts his grandfather made for him, and the pocket knife Boyce gave him, manufactured red, so he wouldn't lose it.

"What freedom I had," Steve recalls. *"I'd get up in the morning, play in the woods, or in the river making little waterwheels, or get on my horse and ride all day. I had nothing to worry about, no worries about what things cost. No bills to be paid. I was totally carefree."*

During these years Steve forged an abiding bond with Montana that defined the basis of his philosophy. *"My philosophy of life is one of adaptation, to be able to function regardless of your means in life"*, he says. Reeves speaks of the appeal for a simple life, free from material demands, and the search for a balanced wellbeing. *"I can live in a little tent somewhere and be very happy in the outdoors, with the fresh air and all."*

In later years, facing both disappointments in Reeves' bodybuilding career and the challenges in Hollywood, these belief systems formed during his childhood would help sustain him.

In the late spring of 1930, Edith Boyce died. At the time of her death the Boyce household was suffering financial difficulties and was made more severe by the Great Depression. In danger of losing his ranch, Stephen Boyce confronted his sister Goldie and told her he could no longer offer support for her and Steve.

Again, Goldie was forced to move. Unable to secure a job in Scobey, she left for Great Falls, a two-day trip at that time. Almost immediately she and a new friend, Frances Chamberlain found work at The Rainbow Hotel. She and Steve stayed with Johnny and May Orva, a couple who had befriended the young widow and her son. While Goldie waited tables at The Rainbow May Orva cared for Steve, and that fall he enrolled into kindergarten.

Although the Orva's continued to be generous about housing Goldie and Steve, she knew by her second year there in Great Falls that it was time for her to make other plans. Reviewing the classifieds everyday she finally spotted an ad placed by a wealthy physician in the community for a job position of a cook. The offer paid well and included living quarters, but the doctor insisted his employee be single and without children. Goldie did the only thing she thought possible for a young, impoverished widow. She took the job and with a guilt that would shadow her for years enrolled seven-year old Stephen into *The Montana Deaconess School*, a boarding school in Helena, two-and-a- half hours southwest of Great Falls.

For the next three years, until he was ten, Steve lived there, seeing his mother only on Christmas and Thanksgiving when he would make the long trip by Greyhound to Great Falls.

His memories of that time are a mixture of loneliness, boredom with school, and fun with new friends. He won $5 in a poetry-reading contest, dug tunnels with pals Johnny Roach, Richard Riley and the Bower brothers, and avoided schoolwork. *"I hated homework back then,"* Reeves recalls. *"Always did. I didn't want to be inside studying when I could be outside playing army."* Because of his lack of interest in school, Steve stayed back in the third grade. *"I was furious,"* he says, *"but I was the only one to blame."* Teachers commented that he was bright, but lazy in class. Preferring to daydream of being a Forest Ranger or cowboy, as he could not envision a future beyond the boundaries of Montana.

The next two years passed uneventfully. Steve spent winters in Helena, and summers on his Uncle Earl's ranch in Big Sandy, just southwest of Havre. He was an active and curious boy always exploring and riding horses. Reeves was quick thinking too. Part of the family lore is a story of how at eight years old he rescued his twin cousins from a charging bull. While Violet and

Viola froze, Steve tossed them on a horse, jumped on himself, and the three galloped away just as the bull roared by. It was a feat that uncannily foreshadowed the *Herculean* deeds adoring fans would years later see him perform on movie screens around the world.

In 1936, Goldie made a move that would mark the end of his boyhood. That summer, she received a letter from Frances Chamberlain, her friend from The Rainbow Hotel. Frances had moved to Oakland, California and in her letter, she encouraged Goldie to follow her, telling her of the great employment opportunities and offering to let Goldie and Steve stay with her until they could find an apartment.

Once again, Steve was uprooted. This time leaving his grandfather, his friends and his treasured Montana outdoors, everything that was familiar and loved for the distant state of California.

Reeves striking his iconic Hercules pose at age seventeen, some fourteen years prior to starring in *Hercules*. Courtesy Steve Reeves

CHAPTER TWO

Oakland

"You can't say enough good about Ed Yarick. He was like a father to Steve."

-Goldie Reeves

The boy who arrived in Oakland, California that August day in 1936 was a lanky, slightly pigeon-toed, bespectacled ten-year-old with a Dutch cut, whose Montana accent immediately pegged him as an outsider. In the eight years that lay ahead he was to undergo a metamorphosis so dramatic it would be unequaled during any other period of his life. By 1943, Steve had transformed himself into a confident, imposing bodybuilder so strikingly handsome he was periodically mistaken for a movie star, and with an extraordinary physique so perfectly proportioned that it electrified the bodybuilding community, and forever after changed the sport.

But that August afternoon in Oakland when he disembarked from the Northern Pacific coach not even the most imaginative bystander catching sight of the shy boy could have conceived of the amazing transformation to come.

No sooner had they stepped out on the platform when Goldie caught site of Frances and George Chamberlain. The friends rushed toward each other, reuniting in a flurry of hugs and kisses. At his mother's prompting, Steve shook hands with George and stood still for a hug and kiss from Frances. After the initial greeting, George carried their luggage to his car. Steve, with a ten-year-old boy's fascination for cars, checked out the gray sedan. A Chevy, of course as Chamberlain worked for the American made company.

It was decided that Goldie and Steve would live with the Chamberlain's until Goldie could find employment and get established in a place of her own. As the four of them headed directly for the outskirts of the city, Steve settled into the car's back, plush seats and got ready for the next leg of their adventure. Immediately Goldie began a nonstop conversation with Frances, bringing her friends up to date on their life, confiding details of the brief vacation she and Steve had taken to Victoria and British Columbia with her then fiancé Wade Owens, and her subsequent break-up with the Montana man. Steve cut in once to tell George about their train trip to Oakland including the amazing ride through the immense Great Salt Lake, then, while the women talked, he pressed his face against the window and scanned the countryside passing by.

The Chamberlain's lived in the Oak Knoll community on the edge of Oakland and in the late 1930's this area was still rural in character, with rolling fields and horse farms. Almost at once Steve felt at home. In many ways, this new terrain was surprisingly similar to the beloved Montana landscape he had left behind.

For Goldie, particularly, this was an emotional time. The years she had lived apart from Steve had been difficult. Although she believed she had no choice, as she had always felt guilty about leaving her son with her parents, and later, at *The Deaconess Boarding School*.

Goldie with Steve during their 1936 summer road trip. Courtesy Steve Reeves

"*Golden really loved that boy,*" her brother Claire Boyce recalled years later in an interview. *"He was the only thing that really mattered to her."* Now they would be a family again.

It was the prospect of being reunited with Steve that had led her to uproot the two of them from the only place they had ever known and move to California. For months, Frances had been writing enthusiastic letters emphasizing the booming economic climate and the opportunities for employment in her home state. However, after several weeks of job hunting, Goldie was encountering a difficult reality. Again, and again she returned home from a futile day of interviews. Finally, after answering a newspaper advertisement for a position as a live-in housekeeper, she was hired by a wealthy family in Napa, a town some thirty-five miles to the north. Her new employer had only one room for the help with no space for children, but the Chamberlain's immediately offered to keep Steve with them so that Goldie could take the job.

In a pattern very much like the years in Great Falls, she and Steve were once again to be separated. She left with a heavy heart, promising to come back every other week to spend time with her son, a commitment she would keep for the next three years. The split was not as traumatic as it might have been. For one thing, the Chamberlain's embraced Steve into their family and treated him like a son. Today, sixty years later, Steve remembers with fondness the years he lived with the Chamberlain's. He can still picture the special space created there for him, an outbuilding in the back yard once used as a spare workshop that George fixed up with running water and a toilet. The ten by twelve-foot room was similar to a bunkhouse, and it delighted young Steve.

"It was a great place for me." Reeves recalls. *"It was a peaceful place."* He made the shed into his personal fort, a location he thanked George very much, and cherished immensely.

He fit into the Chamberlain family with ease and quickly grew to like Oakland. Within days, he discovered a local horse stable and he spent a large amount of time there, delighted to be riding again, to talk with the trainers, to be allowed to groom the horses.

As September approached, Frances enrolled him into The Oakland Elementary School. According to his Montana school records, he had stayed back in the third grade but before he was placed in the fourth level, school officials wanted to test him. When he scored high for his age they arranged for him to skip a year, and that fall he entered the fifth grade.

He made friends quickly, but right from the start the other boys singled him out as a newcomer. He was different and did not talk or act like they did. They had a nickname for him, 'The Foreigner'. *"It never bothered me,"* Steve recalls. *"I just told them that I was a cowboy from Montana, and that the rest of my family were also cowboys."*

Steve earned pocket money by delivering Sunday papers by covering the route on his bicycle. Reeves was now biking all around Oakland and investigating other neighborhoods. Many of his new friends lived in East Oakland and after school, or on the weekends he would ride over to play, often carting his classmates around on the handlebars. His paper route in East Oakland, was the same set of roads that his school bus took him each day from Oak Knoll to Oakland Elementary. On this same road there was one particular two-mile uphill stretch that always gave Steve a difficult time. *"Every time I rode up it,"* Steve remembers, *"I would say to myself, 'either I'm going to make it up this hill, or I won't!' Well, one of three things would happen. One, I would make it to the top successfully. Two, I would quit, which I tried my hardest never to do. Or three, I would snap the chain on my bike from pedaling so hard. Usually, either I would make it to the top, or end up snapping the chain."*

Even then, at age twelve, Reeves' driving force, the source of his motivation was not external, but rather internal. He intuitively understood the secret of individual incentive: identify on a goal and fixate on it! This distinguishing characteristic was his life-long personal method of operation.

"Being extremely focused and narrowing my concentration on a particular point is what has enabled me to succeed at winning things in my life," Steve acknowledges today. *"When I'm out to get something, I always look for a light at the end of the tunnel. Normally, I see it, but if I don't, forget it, I won't make it."*

The story of biking up that Oakland hill would follow him for years, eventually becoming a part of *'The Reeves Legend.'* Even today, the myth is perpetuated as admirers and rivals continue to insist that all of his biking was the sole reason for his astonishing calf development, but Steve himself believes his calves are simply the gift of genetics on his father's side.

In 1939, Goldie returned to Oakland permanently. The previous year the Chamberlains had introduced her to Earl Maylone, a repairman for the Oakland telephone company. After a year of courtship, Earl proposed to Goldie and she accepted. The following week, Steve moved in with his new step-father at Earl's rented home at 1477 76th Ave., East Oakland, a modest, two-bedroom residence in a quiet neighborhood.

Steve had conflicting emotions about his mother's decision to marry. As long as he could remember it had just been the two of them. Then, there was this. While it was tough not to like Earl, as he was a hardworking, popular man and a practical joker who laughed a lot, but Steve wanted a strong father figure. Earl was a thin, wiry man, five feet five inches tall, the complete opposite in stature and looks to everything Steve had ever heard about his real father Lester. Clearly, Earl could not be his role model.

Steve's East Oakland home at 1477, 76th Ave., and Reeves standing beside their neighbor's house, 1940. Author photograph, and Steve Reeves photo.

Then too was Earl's smoking and drinking habits that posed a problem for both Goldie and Steve. Earl smoked several packs of cigarettes each day, and after work he would go down to the local bar and drink until it was time to go home for dinner.

"Earl was the kind of guy to buy everyone at the bar a round of drinks, and he would end up coming home with only half his paycheck!" Steve recalls. *"My mother knew she had to change Earl, or else we would all be broke."*

Goldie wanted a family, and now that she had one she wasn't about to lose it. She was a fighter, so she devised a simple plan. At five o'clock, Goldie would be waiting at the front door with Earl's slippers, a small glass of wine and a warm dinner in the oven. Once Earl changed his habits things became more stable.

That year, to help out his mother with expenses, Steve expanded his paper route to a seven-day delivery. Even though he gave most of his earnings to Goldie, he put aside a little for himself. Like his friends, he enjoyed reading comic books, but his favorite pastime was going to Saturday matinees and watching action adventure films. Every weekend he absorbed the power and mythology of the giant heroes projected on the movie house screens. As a boy growing up in Montana, Steve had always dreamed of being a forest ranger or rancher, but as he watched Gary Cooper in *Plainsman*, Clark Gable in *Test Pilot,* and Johnny Weissmuller swinging from limb to limb in *Tarzan* the dreams of becoming a Hollywood male lead actor had now begun.

In September 1941, Steve entered his freshman year at Castlemont High School. During this time, junior high school in Oakland consisted of three years, leaving three years of high school. That first year was typical of any freshman experience. Like so many other underclassmen, Steve tried to see just where he fit in. Occasionally, he played sports and enjoyed tossing a football with some of his other classmates after school but was never inclined to play organized sports.

The summer after Reeves' second year in high school took on a new, and unexpected direction. Often times, Steve and his other friends would arm wrestle to determine who was the strongest. Inevitably, Reeves ended up the winner, but one day a new player entered the scene. As a sophomore Steve was now getting taller and gaining more weight. Confidently, Steve sat opposite Joe Gambino, a 5'5" kid who weighed no more than 125 pounds. The two locked standard hands in arm wrestling pose and within seconds Gambino had pinned Steve's wrist to the table, defeating Reeves decisively. His ego was bruised and wondered why with his advantage in physical size was not able to beat the smaller kid. Not many days later the mystery was solved when Steve went over to Gambino's house. When Steve asked for Joe, his sister explained that Joe was out back working out. *"Working out? What the heck is that?* Steve recalls. When a bewildered

Reeves went around the house, Joe's source to his strength was immediately revealed. There, right in the middle of the garage, Gambino had set up a weight gym complete with barbells, dumbbells, and stacks of iron plates. Tacked to the walls were photos of various professional bodybuilders. Copies of *Strength and Health* littered the floor. The sixteen-year old Steve made an immediate visceral connection. *"Can I work out with you?"* he asked his friend. *"Sure,"* responded Joe with a grin. *"For twenty-five cents a session."* The young entrepreneur guaranteed that his workouts lessons would include a series of specific exercises with instructions on how to do them.

This arrangement lasted about a week. *"That twenty-five cents per session just became too expensive for me,"* recalls Steve. *"After one week I felt it was time for me to get my own weights and use what little knowledge Joe had taught me and to create my own gym."* He managed to buy a used set of weights from an upperclassman at *Castlemont High*, but before he could set up his equipment at home, he had to convince Earl that he needed to take over the one-car garage. This wasn't easy, but with a little persuasion from Goldie, Earl eventually agreed.

Right from the very beginning, Reeves' body responded quickly to weight lifting and for the first time in his life, Steve had found something that he really connected with. He preferred beginning his workouts by performing standard military presses with a one-hundred-pound barbell, and by the end of the second week he was able to do the one-arm snatch with it. Now his attitude changed. He had a skill and hobby that he was ecstatic about, though many, including Earl, could not understand his enthusiasm.

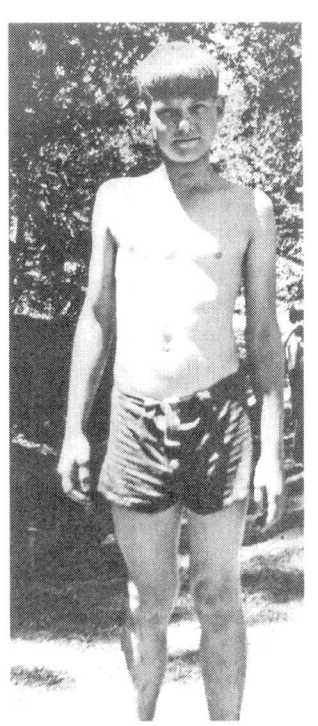 

Steve at age 12, and at age 16. Courtesy Steve Reeves

In 1942, America was largely a nation of spectators, not exercisers. Nobody jogged. No fitness companies such as *Reebok* or *Nike* selling gear, no recumbent bikes. In 1939, Robert M. Hutchins, president of the University of Chicago eliminated football from the program, so it would not interfere with more important pursuits. *"Whenever I feel like exercising,"* Hutchins remarked, *"I lie down until the feeling passes."* Hutchins was the prevailing attitude during this time. The male screen idols of the era were John Wayne, Errol Flynn, and Robert Mitchum, somewhat fit men for the most part, but none of them had any real muscle definition. The majority of the public viewed weight lifting as something not normal.

Of the three high schools in the region Castlemont, Fremont, and Oakland High, Castlemont was the only one that added weightlifting as a part of its physical education program, an unusual choice for that time. Much of its equipment had been donated by The Lions Club fraternal order, and Castlemont boasted more than a thousand pounds of iron and fitness equipment. While Steve preferred to train at home, he absorbed as much as he could from his physical ed teacher regarding proper lifting techniques and form.

Fixing up his own gym became a preoccupation and he was always on the lookout for more equipment, hunting everywhere for additional weights. Usually he came up empty handed. He even went back to Joe Gambino's house to see if his rival wanted to part with any of his equipment but struck out. It was not until a few days later that Steve stumbled across an old cable machine (a weight training resistance devise with pulleys that attaches to a wall). He caught sight of the iron contraption in the back of a salvage metal truck. The vehicle had been making its rounds, going from house to house to collect scrap metal for the ongoing war effort. Apparently one of the local gyms must have thrown the damaged machine on top of the pile. From the instant he saw it perched on top with old stoves and refrigerators, Steve knew exactly what it was and had to have it. Flagging down the driver, Reeves asked how much it would cost to buy the rig. The man winked at Steve and said, *"Make me an offer."* And Steve responded, *"Two dollars?"* Remembers Steve. The driver quickly responded, *"Kid, you got yourself a deal!"*

Now Steve's home gym was really beginning to take shape. Next he built a bench press and a squat rack out of old 2x4's. He covered the floor with some used carpet from the local dump. Instead of eventually losing some-what interest, Reeves' initial enthusiasm for weight training only grew stronger. He worked out every day, often making up his own creative routines which he kept track of by jotting them on the garage wall in black crayon.

Making gains in strength and confidence, Steve soon found that he wanted more than what his home or school gym offered. He wanted to feel part of the bodybuilding world beyond the walls of a converted garage. Again, and again, Steve found himself drawn to a small gym in East Oakland. The address was 3355 Foothill Blvd. The place was *Ed Yarick's Physical Culture Studio*.

Often Steve would stand outside the plate glass window and peer in, trying to imagine what it would be like to be as big and strong as some of the other guys who were training there. Reeves hoped one day that he would get to meet one of them as they left the gym.

At this time, in the early 1940's Oakland was known as the 'Bodybuilding Capital of the World', the mecca of weight training, and it had made its mark in history long before Santa Monica cultivated its well know 'Muscle Beach', and famous *Golds* and *World Gyms*. There were primarily three gyms in the Bay area: *Ed Yarick's Pysical Culture Studio*, *Marks & Paines'*, and *Jack LaLanne's*. Earlier Steve had checked out LaLanne's but Yarick's was only ten minutes from his house by bike, whereas LaLanne's was 45 minutes away.

One day, no longer satisfied with the view through the window, Steve decided to go into Yarick's gym and check it out. As soon as he walked in, he was struck by the intensity of the place. Neither his high school gymnasium, nor his own home gym felt like this place. The sounds and look it gave off were like no other. The clang of iron as it hit the ground thrilled him. The smell wasn't of sweat, but of intensity and will.

At that moment Steve Reeves knew he had found a new home. As Reeves continued to look around with awe, he was interrupted by a rugged blond guy, standing in at six foot-three, 230 pounds. *"Hi,"* the man said. *"I'm Ed Yarick, the owner of the gym. What can I do for you?"*

Steve told Yarick how he admired his gym, and how lifting weights at his house was beginning to become boring. Based on the sincerity he sensed in young Reeves who stood before him, Ed made an intuitive decision. He offered to let Steve train there free of cost to see if he really liked it, an impulsive proposal that would change both of their lives.

Right from the very beginning, Yarick saw something unique in Steve, both in his potential and in his commitment. The entire time Steve trained at his gym Ed never did charge him a dime to work out there. This was the Ed everyone in the bodybuilding community knew, a man known both for his generosity and unselfishness, and for his major contributions to the sport of bodybuilding during these years. He was soon to be the father Steve never had when growing up, the father figure the Montana boy had unconsciously been seeking for years.

Even Goldie recognized the importance of Yarick in Steve's life. *"You can't say enough good about Ed Yarick,"* she once told a reporter. *"He was like a father to Steve, and he got fantastic results with the boys."*

In 1995, Reeves recognized the role Yarick played in his life when he dedicated his book, *'Building The Classic Physique The Natural Way'* to his mentor. *"He was,"* Steve wrote, *"a giving*

Interior photo at *Ed Yarick's Physical Culture Studio* in East Oakland, 1940s. Courtesy Bob Weidlich

person of great integrity and had a terrific sense of humor. Yarick was too young to be my father and too old to be my brother, but he did a real good job at doubling at both. Ed was the nicest guy I have known, and the best friend I ever had."

That day, Steve started working out at Ed's and Earl got his garage back. The next day Steve brought all of his equipment down to Yarick's so there would be more for everyone to use, a gesture that really impressed Ed. Again, he saw Steve's dedication and will to succeed.

The first time Steve started working out at Yarick's, he weighed 163 pounds. His neck was 13.5 inches, his chest 37.5 inches, his waist 28 inches, and his thighs 22 inches. His calves were an astonishing 16 inches.

Reeves soon fashioned a schedule that had him at Yarick's three days a week, for about an hour and a half for each session. Under Ed's tutelage, he concentrated on his whole body in each workout. He believed that it was more beneficial when trying to promote growth to train the entire body in a single intense workout, and then rest on off days, a regime Steve maintains to this day.

The advances the young bodybuilder made were phenomenal. Within four months he had gained a solid 30 pounds. He put on muscle, recognized by other builders in the gym like a sculptor adding clay to his work.

"Actually, building a physique came very easy to me," Steve says. *"The first month I started working out, my body weight stayed at 163 pounds, but my physique really hardened up. A month later I weighed 173. The following month, I hit 183 and the next month I went up to 193. I put on 30 pounds of solid muscle in four months! And that was without any kind of substance assistance (anabolic steroids). The most risque thing we ever took back then was brewer's yeast and Knox gelatin. In fact, after four months, I was the best-built guy at the gym, and there were guys there who had been training for well over three years. However, it took me another year to get from 193 to 203 pounds."*

In a recent article in *IronMan* magazine Reeves said, *"...I didn't know that it was supposed to be difficult to build this muscle, or that muscle. I didn't think of the possibility of failure and not making good progress, and things like that. You know, I saw pictures of guys in muscle magazines and I thought, 'Why not? Why shouldn't I look like that in a few months?"*

Today Reeves is occasionally asked whether or not he took steroids, especially during this time in his life during rapid growth. Reeves full opposition to steroids is clearly evident and confided that he never used steroids on any level. *"There are definitely some things I don't like about bodybuilding today,"* he recently told a reporter. *"One is the use of steroids in the sport. Bodybuilding has gone from being a health-oriented sport, to a steroid sport. I never used steroids, and if they had been available when I first started out, I would not have used them, not in a thousand years!"*

While his drive and dedication were major factors in his rapid development, Ed Yarick played a key role as well. Ed was a thoughtful bodybuilder, a man who was never afraid to try new methods of training. He encouraged Steve to think for himself and to discard some of the established training methods favored by others, and to stick with regimes that worked for Steve's physique and personal diet.

Goldie as well provided Steve with the much-appreciated encouragement and support. She taught him good nutrition and served him only the healthiest of foods, including ample amounts of fresh fruit and dairy products. Whether Earl understood it or not, Goldie realized that her son had found something special in the gym, and although it wasn't clear where it would lead him, she lent her support without question.

Goldie was not alone in recognizing the potential for her son Steve. The world renowned, popular television fitness legend, Jack LaLanne remembers spending time with Steve during these years in Oakland. LaLanne later gained national fame with his television series *The Jack LaLanne Show*, a daily program aired on ABC that promoted physical fitness to all of America, long before

Jane Fonda or Richard Simmons hit the scene. The syndicated program, supported by a devoted following, lasted from 1951 to 1983 and was carried by two hundred stations across the country. During this time LaLanne and his wife Elaine also published a number of books on fitness and nutrition and franchised more than one hundred gyms nationally. In 1943 when he first met Steve, LaLanne was part of a large crowd of bodybuilders who would gather at Washington Park and Sunny Cove to sun bathe and discuss health, nutrition, and weight lifting.

"The first time I met Steve," LaLanne recalls, *"he immediately struck me as a shy and quiet kid, but he possessed a physique that was unbelievable, especially for someone of his age. Steve showed incredible knowledge, even at sixteen, about anatomy, what exercises worked best for what muscles, and he showed incredible will to develop the perfect physique through developing correct symmetry. He also had an incredible enthusiasm for working out, even on his off days when he was supposedly recuperating from his last work-out. He was definitely a hard worker in and out of the gym. You really could see that Ed Yarick was playing a big part in his developing years. Steve talked about Ed like he was his father. Ed kind of took Steve under his wing and taught him the ropes. But what I remember most of all about Steve was how he just loved to work out!"*

By 1943, Steve began showing a sort of cocky side to him. He had just turned seventeen and was still growing at 6'1" and just over 190 pounds. His confidence and ego were beginning to keep pace with his physical growth, resulting in his first fist fight. *"After I started lifting weights, I guess I got pretty sure of myself and let some of the other guys know that I was not going to put up with any of their bullying,"* Steve recalls. *"Well, one day while outside during gym this one guy, who had a reputation as being a bully began pushing some of the others around. When nobody else could take him on, a couple of guys said, 'Yeah, if you think you're so tough why don't you take on Steve? Before I knew it, we were throwing fists left and right. It only lasted a few seconds, but we both got in some good shots. All I got out of that was a bloody nose and the knowledge that I wasn't cut out to be a boxer. That was my first and only fight."*

That same year he took on a part time job. With their parent's permission, students at *Castlemont* were allowed to attend classes during the mornings and work the rest of the day. The nation newly at war was gearing up for the war effort. The shipbuilding industry was constructing a ship, every four days. Employment was easy to find, and Steve found work as a laborer for the Quarter Master Supply Depot in East Oakland. His job required him to transport crates and cargo from loading docks and to storage warehouses, just the kind of heavy work he was looking for. Mornings he would attend his classes at *Castlemont* and after lunch he would work from 1 to 5pm at the Supply Depot. On Monday's, Wednesday's, and Friday's he would finish the day at Ed's gym working out from 6 to 7:30pm.

His social life was also heating up. Still a bit shy with girls, he found himself attracted to Peggy Luwellan, an attractive blue-eyed blond. Although his schedule permitted him very little time for social life, he dated her when he could, mostly on a Saturday night's. One day he asked Peggy to attend a gymnastic meet held at *Castlemont*. While the other students were commenting on the athletic feats of the performers, Steve was studying the other competitor's physiques. A team member from the opposing school particularly impressed him. The athlete had a terrific upper body but lacked the leg development. Watching from the audience, Steve thought, *"If I had his upper body and my legs, or if he had my lower body with his great upper body, then we would both be well built."* After the meet concluded, Steve introduced himself.

Steve at age 17 showing impressive gains. Courtesy Steve Reeves

The gymnast with massive arms and shoulders but underdeveloped legs introduced himself as Jack Delinger, the same Jack Delinger who later became a world-famous bodybuilder noted for his massive legs. After that day, the two of them trained together often times at Ed's gym, and years later ended up becoming very good friends down at Santa Monica's Muscle Beach.

Going into his final year at *Castlemont* Steve was at his heaviest body weight. At 205, the eighteen-year old found himself in demand with every varsity coach from football, baseball, and to basketball asking Reeves to try out for their team. He was flattered by their attention, but between his part-time job down at the Quarter Masters Supply Depot, working out at Ed's three days a week, and dating Peggy, Steve didn't have much time for organized varsity sports.

His pride in weight training and everything it had done for him were evident, and consequently he was astounded when the football coach told him that lifting weights would have to stop if he was going to want to play varsity football. Weight lifting was a terrible thing for the body, the coach said, and was definitely out of the question if anyone hoped to play competitive sports.

Steve knew that working out was the best thing that had ever happened to him, and he couldn't wait to tell Ed, and the guys at the gym what this coach said to him.

"Back then when I was going to high school, they would not even allow football players to swim," Laughs Steve. *"The coaches said it would make the player's muscles to soft and limber. Weightlifting and bicycling were also out because they also said it would tie up your muscles. As difficult as it was to believe weightlifting, cycling and swimming were all forbidden back then for any athlete who wanted to play a sport."*

Bob Weidlich, a classmate friend of Steve's at *Castlemont High School* who also later became training partners of Reeves spoke of his memories back then of Steve. *"He was always a shy kind of person, who kept to himself. Even in high school I remember people used to think he was even kind of dense. But he wasn't at all. People just didn't know Steve because he didn't let them know him. And when it came to grades, he was your average 'B' student just like the rest of us. I guess we didn't really try as hard as the other kids did at homework and studying, mainly because we all worked half days at part-time jobs down at the docks."*

Reeves' senior year went quickly. He never did join the football or baseball team, but he did continue to lift weights at Yarick's, never missing a session. Just before graduation, Steve's class had a picnic celebration for everyone at the local park. That afternoon, many of the seniors got their first look at the astonishing development of their shy classmate. Even at current reunions, classmates talk about the stir he caused that day. The night before the picnic, Steve had decided that he was going to finally show off what he had been working for during the past two years. He arrived late, long after the others had been there for some time, playing volleyball and cooking barbecue. Steve orchestrated his arrival, much like he did later on to draw attention at professional competitions.

Gone were the loose-fitting shirts and baggy slacks. For this occasion, he had dressed in tight Levi's and a T-shirt a size too small, chosen to accent his physique. Immediately, activity stopped. While the guys looked on, all the girls ran up to Steve, circling around him, enticed as if he were a matinee idol or popular singer instead of their quiet classmate. At that moment, Steve knew he liked the attention of being recognized.

A page from Steve's 1944 Castlemont High School year book. Courtesy Steve Reeves

On June 14, 1944, Reeves graduated from *Castlemont* High. For some time, he had been contemplating his future. He knew that he wasn't ready for college. Although Ed had told him many times that he believed Steve was ready for competitive bodybuilding, Reeves had something else in mind.

For months, it seemed that everywhere he looked, Steve ran into Uncle Sam posters stating, *'I Want You! For U.S. Army'* and knew that our country needed him. The choice seemed inevitable, so Reeves went down to the local Army recruiter's office and enlisted. In September, he would begin basic training. For now, he had his final weeks of freedom to enjoy.

During this time Steve met Clancy Ross, a Bay area bodybuilder who went on to become 1945 Mr. America. *"The first time I ever met Steve was at Sunny Cove in Alameda, just outside Oakland,"* Ross recalls. *"I was going there to relax and find a quiet place to lie in the sun. The place was always open back then because it was starting to become run down. The swimming pools were all cracked, and there were no life guards anymore. Well, across the way from where I was, I saw this tall guy, with the widest of shoulders, walking over to me. His legs were also incredible, and his thighs - well they were like pickle barrels - perfectly symmetrical in shape. They had an over-all size and proportion unlike most thigh muscles. He was just thick all the way around! He must have been all but eighteen-years of age because he told me that he was about to join the military. When I witnessed him walking over to me that day, his physique had that perfect V shape to it. And his looks, well they were out of this world!"*

In Oakland, Reeves began his summer job working for the Del Monte Cannery, a job not unlike the one he had held at the Quarter Master Supply Depot. He also moonlighted as a flanger at the shipyard, earning .85 cents an hour. The shipyard job required Steve to fit steel plates onto ship hulls. He would hold large, steel plates up into position while a welder would spot weld them into place. It was the kind of heavy work he always liked.

Later that summer, before he left for Army basic training, Steve went on one last trip with a friend by the name of Clem Poechmann, who at the time worked as a manager at Jack LaLanne's gym. Clem, a twenty-two-year old bodybuilder, shared many of Steve's interests. He knew Reeves was about to leave for the Army, so he invited him to join him and a few others up north to a vacation spot for a few days.

Decades later Poechmann would recall this trip in Milton T. Moore Jr.'s self-published photo booklet *Steve Reeves: A Tribute*, a compilation of hundreds of photos and quotes. *"Perhaps my most poignant memory of Steve was when he and a bunch of us took a bus up to a very popular summer spot on the Russian River called Rio Nido."* Clem said.

Eighteen-year old Steve poses at Sunny Cove Recreation Park in Alameda.
Courtesy Steve Reeves

"We all rented rooms at a motor court and spent the day canoeing, swimming, and sun tanning. Engrossed with the scenery, our activity, and conversation, we didn't realize that many pairs of eyes had been watching us all day. That evening we all attended a dance. We entered the large hall which was in the middle of a huge grove of redwoods, walked over to rows of benches, and sat down waiting for the music to start. When the music began, suddenly girls appeared from everywhere and converged just around Steve, sitting on either side of him, and one even sat on his lap, all of them looking at him admiringly. We didn't know any of them and had not even spoken to any of them. All that attention was just too much. Steve jumped up without speaking a word and left the building. He wasn't scared, just confused and inexperienced. He still didn't consider himself anything special, set apart, or unique. We all stayed at the dance, and when we all arrived back at the room a couple of hours later, Steve was sleeping peacefully. I remember how he looked then in his sleep. Here was a guy who looked better in sleep - just lying there relaxed and undisturbed - than do all of the millions of would-be bodybuilding idols when they are on a stage - trained, tanned, oiled, and tensed. And I remember thinking to myself, 'what a waistline on that guy, what fantastic bone-structure, what symmetry!' Unrehearsed, and not conscious of being looked at that was the scene there that night at the Russian River many, many years ago. I never mentioned it to Steve, but even then, I knew that Steve Reeves was destined to attain heights where no man has stood before, or since."

That summer marked the end to Steve's boyhood. His final days at home in Oakland went quickly before departing for U.S. Army boot camp.

Those days passed too swiftly for Goldie. From the moment she had learned of his enlistment, she had worried continually. She was terrified of losing her only son. The very thought of being a Gold Star mother sent her into a panic, but on September 12th, she smiled bravely and saw Steve off to War.

Corporal Reeves, U.S. Army 1946. Courtesy Steve Reeves

CHAPTER THREE

South Pacific

"My company was involved in the taking of Balete Pass, which in turn exposed me to the horrors of warfare for the first time."

-Steve Reeves, Valley Center, Ca. 1993

      Reeves arrived at Camp Roberts Army base in Paso Robles, California ready for his next challenge - military basic training. With almost three years of intense work outs and bodybuilding at Yarick's under his belt Reeves felt fully prepared for the rigors of boot camp, unlike many of his fellow recruits.

      "When we would set out to do a twenty-mile hike," Reeves recalls, *"many times I would find myself at the head of the company and I would notice that others would be falling out, off to the sides, due to exhaustion."*

      His understanding of how the body worked benefited him greatly. Usually, ten miles into a hike the drill instructor ordered a ten-minute rest. *"It was then that I noticed the entire company chose to sit down"* said Steve. *"I knew from prior training that this would only slow the blood down from circulating through my legs, so instead, I chose to stand, leaning myself and my heavy pack against a tree."*

Because the country was at war, combat infantry training was intensified during basic training and instead of the additional schooling, which usually followed boot camp, men were immediately sent overseas.

Standing in the back row, third from the left Steve graduates from U.S Army Basic training. Courtesy Steve Reeves

Directly following his three months of boot camp, Reeves received orders for the South Pacific. He was one of sixty-one recruits from his company that was transported to San Francisco to board a Naval troop ship, one of thousands headed for the Philippines.

Once at sea, time seemed to stand still. Anxiety ran high. There was little to do but to go over gear, review training and combat skills, and clean one's rifle. Reeves, along with several other soldiers eager to keep in shape and avoid boredom, performed push-ups, chin-ups and climbed ropes. Meals in the Navy galley were lighter than Reeves was used to and in order to maintain his desired body weight, he devised a plan. Troops were divided into three different shifts for meals, with each man given a card indicating which shift he was to eat at during that particular meal. Reeves had, by this time, made several contacts on board and was able to scam three cards for each of the three meals every day. This meant nine meals every twenty-four hours. His scheme was to dress, comb his hair, and speak a little differently each time he showed up for chow. The strategy worked perfectly, especially for someone who loved to eat.

In early 1945, the naval transport ship arrived at the island of Mindanao. One day, while waiting to sign on with the 25th Division, Company A, Reeves met a small Filipino man outside the base who knew where he could find and sell him, of all things, an iron bar barbell set. Steve jumped at the chance for ten U.S. dollars.

Using his new equipment, Reeves refined his work-out so that it was productive even though the amount of poundage was much lighter than at Yarick's. In the process he learned even more about the importance of form and style.

"Since I had less than 100 pounds to work out with I had to make the most of what I had," recalls Steve. "I performed my reps very slowly, with deep concentration, and would perform as many repetitions as I could. I found that not only did I get a great *cardiovascular workout from doing my squats this way, but my leg gains were also very good. At the end of the time I trained in the Philippines, I was doing 100 reps in a row without pausing - with about 100 pounds on my back (which was approximately half of my body weight) - in squats!"* When he finally received his orders to the front line, Reeves took the weights with him.

The 25th Division was sent directly into battle. *"My company was involved in the taking of Balete Pass, which in turn exposed me to the horrors of warfare for the first time,"* Steve recalls. *"In order not to become devastated by the death and destruction I witnessed going on all around me, I would try and detach myself mentally from what was going on,"*

Reeves writes in *'Building The Classic Physique, The Natural Way.'* *"...I began to look at myself as an observer, and not as a participant in the action. I saw men killed and soldiers carried out on stretchers on a daily basis. I was able to remain calm by distancing myself from what was going on and by forming vivid mental images of myself being anywhere but where I was."*

Steve remained on the front line until June of 45', when at that point he contracted malaria and dengue fever. So severe were the illnesses that for the next seven months Reeves had monthly recurrences and, as a result experienced a sudden loss of body weight, dropping from 200 to 175. After two months in a small hospital near the front, Reeves was transferred to the Quartermasters Corps where he awaited new orders.

In September after the allied occupation of Japan, Reeves received his final command post at a military base in the small town of Otaru, on the isle of Hokkaido. With the war nearly over Reeves found himself performing numerous non-combatant duties. He conducted weight training for officers during the day, and at night tended bar at the 'O' club. With just under a year of his two-year enlistment service obligation remaining, Steve began the journey back to his original state of fitness.

"*During my long illness, I had no chance whatsoever to train with weights,*" Reeves says. "*And as sick as I was, I unfortunately had very little incentive. However, while in Japan I began to feel like myself again. With the war now over and with a new lease on life, I decided to do something about my physique once more.*"

After tracking down an interpreter, Steve located a Japanese steel foundry. With well, drawn out diagrams, and specific measurements, Reeves had the foundry make him a 210-pound barbell set for which he paid one hundred U.S dollars. Upon forging, Reeves proudly stored the custom weight set under his cot in his barracks, and the home-made bench press he made ironically passed Army inspection due to its resemblance to an ironing board. Soon his work outs were back in full swing, and he had regained weight again, now at a respectable 195 lbs.

Standing alongside troops aboard the U.S.S Waterbury, Reeves returns home from war. Courtesy Steve Reeves

In early September, having survived war and illness along with his military experience behind him, Reeves boarded the USS Waterbury in Yokohama and headed home, one of the thousands of soldiers returning to a grateful nation.

Steve back at Yarick's Gym training for the 1946 Mr. Pacific Contest. Courtesy Steve Reeves

CHAPTER FOUR

The Iron Game

"My passion was not narcissism, it was a sense of accomplishment."

-Steve Reeves, 1993

    The Reeves who returned from the Philippines in 1946 was far from the man who had enlisted in 1944. When he disembarked at the Oakland Ship Yards that September and jumped on a local bus for home, he was momentarily without goals. Certainly, there was no way he could have envisioned that within seven months he might be crowned Mr. America, the youngest man ever to win the title. The idea of such a victory was so remote, so far-fetched and removed from reality that it was not even a dream.

    Although money was not an immediate problem, as throughout Steve's two-year tour he had sent his paycheck back home with instructions for Goldie to buy U.S. War bonds. Reeves had no prospects. More so, he had no real direction, not even a girlfriend, nothing to ground him or hold the promise of a future. Instinctively Steve knew exactly what he needed to get himself back on track. Shortly after his arrival home, he headed for 3355 Foothill Boulevard. Nothing had changed. Not the sprawling letters on the window proclaiming *'Ed Yarick's Physical Culture Studio'*, not the sounds of clanking iron, nor the smell of sweat. Everything was so immediately familiar, as if Steve had only been away for weeks, and not years. When Ed caught sight of Steve, he greeted Reeves like a returning son, teasing him with a standard Yarick line *"You look great. Who's your undertaker?"* and then inviting him over to the house for one of Alyce's home cooked meals. Now Steve felt as if he really had returned home.

That first day he began training again. Determined to regain his pre-enlistment physique, Steve started with a five-minute stretching routine, then reached for the barbell and began with his favorite opening set: Behind-the-neck military presses. Although he was no clearer about his future, he found comfort in the gym and quickly regained his focus.

Before his enlistment, Reeves had been Yarick's protege, but now the two worked as gym partners. Their training sessions were marked by a new level of discipline. While lifting, they tolerated no half lifts, or swinging of the weights, no cheating of any kind and held to their golden rule: *"If you cheat, you cheat yourself!"*

Researching every aspect that would improve his training, Reeves incorporated a very strict approach to his diet. While today, nutrition plays a central part in any serious bodybuilder's training, his interest in this area was very innovative for the 1940's, and is credited as the one bodybuilder responsible for getting nutrition consciousness within the sport.

At home, Goldie again encouraged Steve in his efforts and prepared meals according to his new dietary regimen: giant salads, vegetables, fruits of every sort, a quart of milk a day. A typical breakfast for Steve, being the most important meal of the day was four fried eggs, a bowl of wheat cereal with strawberries and cream, four slices of wheat toast with honey and three glasses of goat's milk. By now he was emphatic about eliminating any food containing white flour or refined sugar. *"We had a term for it at the gym."* recalls Steve. *"White death, meaning refined sugar, devitalized white flour, and salt!"* Reeves was insistent on getting nine hours of sleep a night. He drank neither coffee or tea. The worst sin was smoking.

During his first two weeks of training and dieting, Steve's weight jumped from 195 to 215 pounds. His physical and mental conditioning were better than ever. Quite often Yarick would bring up the subject of getting Steve to enter into a physique competition, encouraging him that he is champion material. Although Reeves had never really considered competing, the idea was now beginning to appeal to him.

At this time in 1946, there were three regional bodybuilding competitions being held and sponsored on the West Coast: Mr. California, Mr. Western America, and Mr. Pacific Coast. But before Steve even considered applying for entry, he knew he needed to broaden his understanding of the sport.

Largely, unfamiliar with the practical and aesthetic aspects of bodybuilding competitions, Steve set out to educate himself on every level. In late November, he heard that the Mr. Bay Area contest was being held at the Berkeley Campus of The University of California and decided to see the show for himself as a spectator.

The event was organized by Walt Baptiste who also owned and operated his own gym in downtown San Francisco. Baptiste had hoped to sell 2000 tickets that night, and he did just that, having to turn people away one hour before curtain time. *'Standing Room Only'* read a hastily scrawled sign at the front entrance, and soon even that was removed.

Steve arrived in plenty of time to get a ticket. Never particularly comfortable with large crowds, Reeves was overwhelmed by the turnout and stayed outside the auditorium until it was nearly time for the show to begin.

Joe Corsi was there that night as well. Corsi, a recently discharged wartime Air Force B-24 bomber and physical fitness enthusiast had been working out at *Jack LaLanne's Gym*, and it was LaLanne who suggested that he take in the competition at Berkeley.

"So, I'm in this auditorium and the place is packed!" Corsi recalls. *"It was just like a movie. Everybody yakking and talking so loud that you couldn't even hear yourself think. There had to be more than 2000 people there that night. All of a sudden, just before curtain time everything becomes quiet and everybody's head is turning around. I looked too, of course, and who do I see walking down the aisle but this big, good-looking stud, dressed in dark green Army trousers and a matching wool shirt. A rumble went through the crowd. Everyone was asking, 'Who is that?' It was clear this guy had been working out real hard, too, because nobody looked like that. He was all shoulders and no waist. A good head of hair, handsome guy. He just had that big, raw boned good looks, a real fantastic natural physique. That was the first time I ever saw Steve Reeves."*

Another person who witnessed Steve's appearance that night was Bob Weidlich, Steve's high school friend from Castlemont High. *"Yeah, Steve made quite an appearance that night in Berkeley. I think that was when he got his first taste of stardom. Steve was a sight for sore eyes, I'll tell ya. His looks were out of this world. And his physique was incredible. His shoulders were the widest you could imagine, and his tailored Army shirt tucked tight into his slacks made his shoulders look all the wider. You could have heard a pin drop when everyone started to look back at him."*

Steve was not unaware of the stir he was now creating. *"When I put on that Army uniform the other guys used to call me the shape."* Steve remembers. But within minutes he had blocked out everything in the auditorium except the competition. As the show began, he focused on the contestants, analyzing and evaluating every aspect of their presentation. He critiqued their posing and timing, and how they walked. He watched their routines, instinctively knowing what would work for him, and what would not. Steve obtained an innateness right from the very beginning of his bodybuilding career, that would totally separate him from his other competitors. A winning trait that would ultimately place him at the top of his game and earn him his very own individual, champion style.

The next day he returned to Ed's gym fired up with a new purpose, and a new workout partner. At the Berkeley show, Steve had rekindled his friendship with Bob Weidlich and before they left that night they had agreed to begin training together at Ed's.

In the following days, Reeves and Weidlich worked out religiously, lifting three days a week, two and half hours per workout. Weidlich recalls in a recent interview that their workouts were like clockwork, with each one motivating the other to lift harder and harder so as to achieve their desired goals in body weight and muscularity.

"Steve's metabolism was incredible!" Weidlich remembers. *"He had the perfect chemistry for building muscles. I used to hate it. The two of us would go out for lunch and Steve would eat one hot dog and be able to gain a pound of solid muscle from it. Where as I would have to eat ten hot dogs just to gain the same weight."*

Even in the gym among other dedicated bodybuilders their grueling workouts were legendary. They used to start off with shoulders. Then they'd work the chest using a very wide grip on the bench press as they believed would create that classic V shape that Steve aimed at perfecting. He always prided himself and continually worked to achieve his signature broad shoulder appearance that tapered classically to a narrow waist. This look was set off by well-developed thighs and chiseled calves. From the start, symmetry and proportion were what Reeves always focused on heavily. Muscle development obviously was very important, but never at the expense of symmetry.

After chest workouts, they worked the back, then arms, and then lastly the legs. They wore full sweats. Never a tank top and shorts. This way they could really sweat the fat off. The work outs never lasted at less than two hours, and they didn't spend a minute of time talking or wasting time.

Steve remembers Bob as being the best workout partner he ever had. *"I only had three training partners throughout my career,"* he says. *"And the best was Weidlich. He had a lot of enthusiasm, a lot of drive, and he was built a lot like me, except he was 5 feet, 5 inches."* One of the qualities Steve most appreciated about Weidlich was his dedication. *"He was never the sort of guy who did not feel like working out that day.' He was always up for* training, and I was always motivated for a workout, so we were the perfect training partners."

Reeves also appreciated Weidlich's humor. *"He was always doing something that made me laugh,"* Steve recalls laughing. *"One time, Bob wanted to get into the fire department, but the minimum height requirement was 5 feet 6 inches. So, Bob shaved a section of hair off the top of his head, put a piece of plastic over it, combed his hair back over the plastic and went back to the fire department and measured in at 5 feet 7 inches."*

They had now been working out together for several weeks when Weidlich brought in an advertisement to the gym and handed it to Steve. Sam Loprinzi was sponsoring a Mr. Pacific Coast physique contest in Portland, Oregon, on December 21st, and Weidlich encouraged him to enter, saying if Steve entered, he would too. *"It was kind of a challenge between the two of us,"* recalls Bob. *"A sort of, if you do, I will as well kind of thing."*

Purposely, they kept quiet about their plans, especially to Yarick confiding only to Steve's mother Goldie. A week prior to the contest date they sent in their applications and the $5.00 entrance fee. Immediately, the intensity of their workouts increased. The last session before they left for Portland were so intense that even Ed seemed to be a bit suspicious as to what was going on.

On Friday, December 20th, Steve and Bob boarded a Pacific South Railway car and headed for Portland, Oregon. All they carried with them was a gym bag, a pair of posing trunks, towels and a change of clothes. Goldie had packed sandwiches and fruit for them, enough, she thought, to last the trip, but with nerves and anticipation running so high, the food never lasted much past Redding, some two hours north of Oakland.

To save money they decided to rent a compartment sleeper together. *"We ended up sleeping head to toe."* Weidlich says, laughing at the memory, *"And the way we did it was, I would put two pillows over his feet, and he'd put two pillows over my feet, that way we both could get a good night sleep. But the train was pretty full that night, and all that separated us from the aisle was a sliding curtain. Apparently, Steve was sort of lying over the edge when he was sleeping, because all of a sudden, he must have jumped out of his rack about a foot high because some guy elbowed Reeves in the back yelling, 'Hey, keep your ass out of the aisle and in your bunk!' We just started laughing out loud at the whole idea of that trip."*

On their arrival into Portland they registered at the contest, found a hotel, and tried to keep their nerves at bay.

The competition was a first for Portland, and that night the auditorium was sold out. To warm up the audience, the event began with the popular hand balancing act of Bradly and Merisi. After introducing the judges for the event, Joe Loprinzi, Al Kost, Dud Nelson, George Pavlich and Dr. C Wheeler the announcer explained the event's point system that was going to be used, so as to determine who the winners were going to be in three height classes. Seven points were for proportion, five points for muscularity, two points for posing ability, and one point for general appearance, combining a maximum of 15 points from each of the five judges' scorecards. Seventy-five points would give a contestant a perfect score. The event allowed each bodybuilder their choice of three poses, with a maximum of 90 seconds to complete their routine.

As the lights dimmed, the men waited backstage for their group to be called to the platform. The first set of bodybuilders were the 5 feet and under class, followed by the middle class 5'6 to

5'8. Then finally, the tall men category was announced, and Reeves along with six other contestants took the stage.

    Walking out on to stage for the very first time as a new professional bodybuilder, Reeves felt nervous, and a bit out of place. But when his name was announced, Steve confidently stepped up onto the posing platform and everything he worried about quickly disappeared. (Note: During these early years within the sport of bodybuilding an applicant did not need any requirements to apply and compete, as there were no semi-pro contests. Unlike today, in order to compete on the pro circuit level, every applicant must have first won first place within a recognized amateur contest, thus earning them their pro card advancing them into the pro circuit).

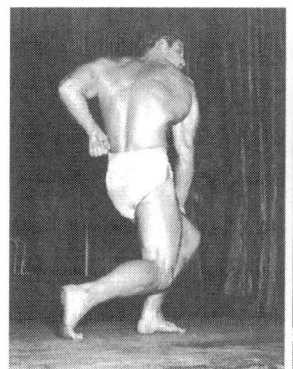 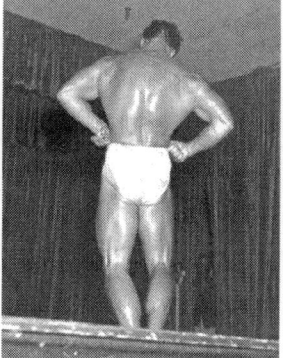 

Steve strikes a series of poses during the final scoring at the 1946 Mr. Pacific.
Courtesy Steve Reeves

    Gracefully, Reeves struck the three poses he had chosen: the front double biceps, the rear double bicep pose, and the front lat spread, a favorite of his that would become one of his trademark poses. The audience responded wildly, cheering and whistling, while off to the sides stagehands peered through the curtains. As the crowd roared louder, Steve smiled more than ever with pride and confidence. Two contestants still waited to pose, but long before the judges handed their score cards to the emcee, the audience knew Steve had taken first place. He scored a near perfect 72 points.

After a brief pause, the emcee called the three winners of each individual class back out onto the platform, to again, pose for the judges, this time for the over-all winner. When the results were announced, 1946 Mr. Pacific Coast went to twenty-year old Steve Reeves from Oakland, California.

A *Strength & Health* magazine caption of a photo for an article on the event labeled the contest winner as *'The Herculean Steve Reeves'* a prophetic designation. His role in global film making as the legendary Hercules was still some eleven years into the near off future.

After his first title win, Steve and Bob (who placed 1st in the short class and 4th overall) celebrated that night in the city of Portland, until late Sunday when they re-boarded The Pacific South Railway back to Oakland. The following day was Christmas Eve, and Steve returned to Ed's gym to resume his training as usual.

Yarick had not heard from Steve or Bob since their last training day the previous Thursday morning, some six days prior. Over the weekend Ed had wondered if Steve was sick, or if he had decided to try out another gym? Yarick was puzzled by Steve's absence because Reeves was in such great shape now that he couldn't understand why Steve would break his training schedule there at Ed's. Before jumping to conclusions, Ed decided to wait and see if Steve would show up on Tuesday. Later he told a local reporter, *"When Steve walked into the gym the following Tuesday, I found out why he'd missed his training sessions. He walked in with this great, glowing grin on his face and said, 'Merry Christmas, Ed!' Then he handed me a huge trophy inscribed, 'Mr Pacific Coast of 1946.'"*

Reeves proudly poses center stage holding his 1946 Mr. Pacific Coast trophy.
Courtesy Steve Reeves

While Yarick was quite surprised by the unexpected manner in which Steve had entered the contest, he was not startled by his victory and began to immediately research for Steve additional contests for his protege. The Mr. California was scheduled for January, but because Steve believed winning the larger Mr. Pacific title made him ineligible, Reeves did not enter.

'Don't worry about it,' said Yarick, who was already aiming for a grander title for Reeves. The 1947 Mr. America contest was slated for June in Chicago. This was the next title Yarick believed was right for Steve to be shooting for now.

Steve training for his second title shot at the 1947 Mr. Pacific Coast. Courtesy Steve Reeves

CHAPTER FIVE

Drive, Desire & Discipline

"I think the mind is extremely important in building muscles. I always had a great communication between the mind and the muscles and concentrated deeply while working out."

- Steve Reeves, 1994

Ed Yarick had a keen understanding of physiology, and a self-taught scientific approach to exercise. He constantly looked for innovative ways at enhancing training methods, both through updated equipment, as well as refining dated workout routines. With Chicago in mind, Ed began to concentrate on ways to better Steve's exercises. He invented a crude example of the first incline bench, knowing its use would isolate the upper chest and give Reeves the increased development in pectorals, including the squared, tapered look in his lower chest that he wanted to improve.

While it was true that Steve had been gifted with a natural physique, the aspects he was to become known for (square pecs, tapered V-shape, sculpted calves, narrow waist) were part of a very conscious vision. Reeves was seeking the Greek ideal of the body under the direction of Yarick who brought an intelligent, analytical application to this quest, an approach that gave Steve an edge over his rival competition. He never performed an exercise unless he understood not only the muscle being worked, but the specific part of that muscle, and to what degree. Reeves knew that the full squat built too much muscle in the upper thighs and buttocks for the look he was aiming for, so instead he chose the hack squat instead. He desired a column-like neck and worked only the exercises which he knew would contribute to this ideal, often using resistance training. Steve disliked the tapered ends he saw in most bodybuilders, so he focused more attention to his calves and forearms.

    Now that he was a title holder, Reeves was getting more recognition in the gym. Other bodybuilders looked to him for advice for training methods and lifting tips in hopes that they too could build an impressive physique such as Steve's. Often, they were persistently interrupting Steve in the middle of his workouts to ask him, training questions. So Weidlich quickly became Steve's deflector saying, *"Look, don't bug the guy. He's concentrating and wants to get the best results from lifting. After our workout, Steve would be happy to assist you, but not during our training."* recalls Weidlich.

    One day a novice lifter from out of town visited the gym for a workout. He saw Reeves working out and sure enough approached him hoping to ask him some training questions. Immediately Weidlich approached him to back him away but the fan continued to interrupt Reeves' with constant questions during their workout.

Steve and Bob exchanged a quick glance. The regulars who caught it smiled and sat back waiting to see what the two practical jokers would do to the persistent visitor.

Steve instead walked up to the guy and told him. *"Here's what you need to do."* Laughs Reeves. *"You have to do three exercises all at once. That is the only way to get in shape."*

"Three at once?" asked the visitor.

"Yeah. That way, you can get through the entire workout in half the time."

Steve motioned for Bob and Ed to help demonstrate. *"I laid prone on the bench,"* Reeves said. *"Bob was working on my traps and neck, Ed was working my thighs with one leg curls, and I was working my deltoids with side laterals, all at the same time."*

"That is what you have to do if you really want to get the best results!" he told the bewildered visitor. Days later, they were still chuckling over the idea of this guy struggling over the three-in-one approach.

A great piece of advice Steve offered many times to others at the gym was the importance of concentration, a quality he believed played a crucial role in the development of muscles, even more than wanting to use heavy weights, verse lighter weight. *"By the end of our workouts,"* recalls Bob, *"Steve and I would literally be melting in sweat, and the thing about it was that Steve would only be using medium sized weights, while I would be using much heavier weight. The frustrating thing for me was that we would be getting the exact same results."*

An Oakland newspaper clipping of Reeves and Weidlich hand balancing for neighborhood fans, 1947. Courtesy Steve Reeves

Reeves had discovered that he could get the same outcome with lighter weights, simply by focusing intensely on the muscle while it was being worked. Long before the technique became familiar, he understood the potential of visualization.

"I believe the mind is extremely important in building muscles," Reeves says. *"My slogan is not 'no pain, no gain', but rather 'no brain, no gain.' I always had a great communication between the mind and the muscle and concentrated deeply while working out. I would not talk to anybody while training, that's how focused I was. When I worked out, I would mentally isolate the muscle being worked, concentrating on it exclusively. I would work the muscle very slowly so that I could really feel the exercise all the way up, and all the way down. The only way you can create that superior line of communication between mind and muscle is through concentration, and by practicing muscle control in your spare time."*

Still in the macho environment of the gym where it was often the magnitude of the amount weight that counted, Steve occasionally felt a little insecure about people knowing that he preferred less poundage.

Yarick, who oversaw Steve's continual and rapid improvement, counseled him to ignore what others thought. *"Steve was a genetic phenomenon and obviously did not have to prove to anyone that he should have been using ninety-pound dumbbells as opposed to 30 or 40 pounders,"* he once told a reporter.

The proof was in the results. This outcome was seen in the mirrors at the very end of the Ed's gym. Weidlich remembers the weekly posing sessions the bodybuilders posed off at in front of these mirrors. *"When we felt we were ready to show off what we had been working really hard for, we would all have some fun with it by having pose downs with each other. To this day, I can still see*

Steve posing back there. There he would stand with that incredible V shape physique. It was awesome!"

Although his focus was on that years Mr. America contest, Steve was also concerned about his future outside the gym. Three months had passed since his discharge and he still had no real job prospects in mind. He knew he couldn't be a bodybuilder for the rest of his life, nor did he want to be. He began to look around for career choices. *"There was a guy by the name of Norman Marks who was a well-known chiropractor, one of the best in California at the time, and there were also other chiropractic offices around the Bay area."* recalls Steve. *"The profession was really taking off. I already knew most of the names of the muscles, and how they functioned, so I thought, well that kind of goes together."*

Under the G.I. Bill which provided educational funds for veterans, Steve enrolled in *The California School of Chiropractics* in downtown San Francisco. It was late January now and he had two goals firmly in mind. In preparation for the upcoming Chicago contest, Steve continued to work out three days a week with Weidlich. Meanwhile, he now attended classes full time in the city. *"I really knew I was on to something with what I was studying."* Says Steve. *"My major was chiropractic's, and my minor was physiotherapy and massage. With physiotherapy one could rehabilitate the body of people who had polio, or various other similar ailments. While with massage one can get the muscles back into shape. I felt 1 was bound to get a job in one of these two fields."* For the first time in his life Steve found school work easy. Because of his keen understanding of the body and how it operates, Reeves was already ahead of his classmates that first semester.

Rather than feeling overwhelmed by his schedule of training and school Steve relished within the challenges. Using his remarkable ability to focus on his goals, Reeves let nothing get in his way. *"Steve had a real will to exceed,"* remembers Weidlich.

"We all knew that one day he was going to be the best in his field, whether it was in bodybuilding, medicine, or even show business. Everyone knew he was going big places. Steve knew it too."

This was not the first time anyone had envisioned Steve as an actor. Recently, on a road trip to Los Angeles, he had been mistaken as a movie star. Reeves had gone down to L.A. for the weekend hoping to check out the scene at Santa Monica's Muscle Beach while visiting Tony Diez, an Army colleague he had toured with while serving in the South Pacific.

On Saturday, when they hopped off the trolley at Muscle Beach, Steve felt immediately at home. The place was a glorified Sunny Cove, just like back in Alameda. The beach and boardwalks were packed with hundreds of people from all the lovely ladies in bikini's, to trapeze artists, hand balancers and gymnasts. Everyone was sun bathing and swimming, and of course there were the bodybuilders and weightlifters who had given the beach its name.

Instantly, Steve attracted another crowd. Unaware that he was already beginning to build a reputation outside of the Oakland area, he was amazed to be recognized as last year's Mr. Pacific Coast. Bodybuilders approached him for advice once again, just like back at Ed's and wondering if he was going to try and retain his title of Mr. Pacific Coast on May 24th.

With his focus directed solely on the Mr. America contest in June, Steve had never considered defending his title, but now the idea intrigued him, especially when he heard that Eric Pedersen, a big-name competitor was entering the contest.

At the time, Pedersen was L.A.'s champion bodybuilder and was training under the tutelage of Bert Goodrich at his Hollywood gyms. Goodrich, a former Mr. America was now a well-known promoter within the fitness field and was the brother-in-law to Vic Tanny, one of the biggest names in the West Coast bodybuilding fraternity. Steve liked the idea of competing against the popular, and many believed favored Eric Pedersen.

On their return from Santa Monica, Reeves and Diez hopped back on the public red trolley. As soon as Steve sat down, another passenger leaned over and asked him, *'Are you a movie star?'* "*No,*" Steve replied smiling, and said impulsively, *"But someday I will be."*

When they reached their stop and exited the trolley, Diez turned to Steve and said. *"Do many people ask you that?"* he asked. *"You know, you really should think about getting into acting someday. You do have the looks for it. You would be great at it!"*

The idea was intriguing, but not practical. Back at home, Steve concentrated on his immediate goals with his schooling in chiropractic's, and particularly his training for the approaching Mr. America contest in Chicago. Still, a broader vision and horizon remained within Steve's ambitions that went far beyond what Oakland had to offer.

Reeves returned from Santa Monica fueled with the idea of competing against L.A.'s favored Pedersen in competition, and in result his training reached a higher degree of intensity. Steve recalls, *"I remember feeling so strong and energetic after those workouts during that year in 47', that I felt as though I could walk up to a parked car and flip it over!"*

At home, Goldie's kitchen became a nutritional laboratory. The Yarick's had given Steve a Swedish speed juicer as well as a Waring blender for making all sorts of juice and vegetable power drinks. *"I had all kinds of fancy recipes,"* Steve recalls smiling. *"Some of them were better than others."*

One day, Steve phoned Weidlich and invited him to stop by his family's house and try a new drink he had just created. *"Steve was like a nutritional chemist there at work in his kitchen,"* laughs Weidlich. *"I remember this one drink he had me try made from avocados, goat milk, entire eggs shells and all, and whatever else he could find to make it interesting. He thought it would be so nutritious, but instead it was horrible! The two of us couldn't even finish it. We ended up pouring it all down the sink!"*

High fluid intake during exercise, and the role it played in metabolism was one of several principles that Steve hit upon that would in time be duplicated by fitness and nutritional experts.

"I automatically did something correctly when I was working out," Reeves says. *"I didn't know what I was doing at the time, but I did it instinctively. I used to drink a lot of water and I would mix lemon and honey with it, and that way I was able to replace all the electrolytes that would be lost through perspiration."* He was doing this forty years before similar products were marketed for athletes, his home-mixed brew a forerunner to today's *Gatorade*.

"Something instinctively told me 'that's the thing to do, I must do it, and I did. By having lemonade, you know, I alkalized the system and I was able to work out more without my muscles getting too much blood in them, too soon. In other words, they would not tire out before they were tired." It was a revolutionary biochemical idea.

Steve incorporated other innovations. He thrived on variety and disliked monotony. He disliked calling his workout routines which to him meant doing the same thing over and over again, but instead called them schedules. And he would frequently, altered them. *"What I liked to do was change my schedules. For example, I would use the same exercises, but maybe one day a week, I would do between 5-7 reps, another day during the week, I would perform between 7-11 reps, and on another day, do 11-15 reps. That way you confuse the body so that it doesn't get into a routine and stay there. The body is used to really exerting for those seven reps, when all of a sudden you hit the body with fifteen reps instead, it now has to change completely. It really works out well."* Reeves says.

He also carried this approach to life itself outside the gym, applying great attention to his overall appearance. Steve brushed his teeth with baking soda and salt, then massaged his gums with the same solution. He experimented with his hair style until he was satisfied that the cut complemented the structure of his face. He cared for his skin, as well. In preparation for the upcoming contests, Reeves incorporated raisins and carrots into his diet, believing that the red in the iron of the raisins and the orange of the carrots worked together to enhance the melanin in his body, thus darkening his tan.

Reeves had a mindset approach he applied to every corner of his life, and he referred it to the three D's; Drive, Desire, and Discipline. These principles were now being applied to his daily routines more so than ever. His preparation now was to compete in two, back to back physique contests, one of which at hoping to defend his title of Mr. Pacific Coast.

Earlier in January, Reeves had passed up the Mr. California contest believing he was ineligible because he had won the larger 1946 Mr. Pacific Coast title the month before.

The 1947 Mr. Pacific Coast was being staged and sponsored by the Southern California Weightlifting Association, scheduled for May 24th at the Embassy auditorium in Los Angeles, with the goal of drawing a maximum capacity audience.

A *Your Physique* magazine article covering the 1947 Mr. Pacific contest. Courtesy Tony Lanza

In the dressing room during the preliminaries, Earle Liederman, a close friend of the legendary bodybuilder Eugene

Sandow, and at the time the world's largest mail-order fitness company got his first glimpse of Reeves.

"Winding my way around and looking over the contestants who were warming up," Liederman said to a reporter, *"I saw a small gathering around a tall, good-looking fella. He looked quite impressive standing there among those youngsters, and almost a head taller than any of them. Here I mused to myself was a real physique standout, not only among the novice group but also among those who were competing in the major contest. Yet, when I heard that he was still in his early twenties, I could not help but marvel at how a young man his age could develop such a great build. Yet there I stood and seeing was believing."*

The caliber of competition in Reeves' class was more impressive that it had been the previous year, with many of the contestants seasoned bodybuilders among the circuit. With only one title win behind him, Steve was the most inexperienced applicant. On the platform next to him were Bill Cantrell, and the well-known Eric Pedersen. Almost at once, it was clear that Pedersen was the hometown favorite, but rather than be intimidated, Steve relished the competition.

At last the emcee called *Number Nineteen,* and Reeves stepped forward. Already, he had developed a distinctly individual style, moving quickly from one pose to another, with dramatic, cat-like grace, but there was something else beyond the impressive body that mesmerized the audience. Steve was a natural showman. When he smiled at the crowd, he radiated enthusiasm, a tremendous vitality and force, and the audience responded with tremendous applause. Within seconds he had captured the devotion they had come prepared to give to his rival Pedersen.

Walt Marcyan, a reporter for *Your Physique* magazine wrote, *"The competition was terrific, but Steve out-glowed, out-*

shone, and 'out-muscled' them all! One personally proclaimed him to be the finest specimen of American Manhood I have ever seen. ...He hasn't a single weak spot in his make-up. Each and everyone one of his marvelous muscles are perfectly developed, and as large as any eye would care to see. He represents the perfect ideal for every bodybuilding enthusiast to desire."

The judges concurred with Marcyan's assessment. *"Retaining his title," said Ed Yarick for* Muscle Magazine, *"Steve earned trophies for Best Arms, Best Chest and Best Legs. Not only had Reeves edged out his rival Pedersen to recapture his Mr. Pacific Coast title, but he ended the night holding four trophies, the most ever won by one competitor at a single show."*

Steve did not allow himself much time to savor his victory. Now he wondered how he would stack up against a national competition. Comparing himself to the two previous Mr. America's Steve personally knew both Clancy Ross (1945), and Alan Stephan (1946), so he felt he had a somewhat realistic shot at the title. On his return to Oakland, Reeves amped up preparations for Chicago.

He began pouring over muscle magazines, studying all the top contenders he would be competing against. He searched for articles on Kimon Voyages, John Farbotnik, and George Eiferman, studied their poses, their physiques, their strong points, but most particularly their weak ones.

.

Reeves accepts his 1947 Mr. Pacific trophy from 1945 Mr. America Clancy Ross. Courtesy Steve Reeves

Mentally, Steve was winning the contest before he even stepped out onto the stage.

Reeves knew he was now ready.

He could not wait for Chicago.

Steve posing at the 1947 AAU Mr. America Contest. Courtesy Tony Lanza

CHAPTER SIX

Mr. America

"We knew Steve had won a few titles on the West Coast, but no one in the Midwest or on the East Coast had seen him. A few days before the contest we heard of rumors about a man who had throngs of people following him along Lake Michigan beach front. We couldn't imagine who could draw crowds merely by walking along a beach in the Midwest, so naturally we were anxious to see this man. Well, when we saw Steve before the competition, we knew he was Mr America without there even being a contest - there was no contest."

-George Eiferman, 1948 Mr. America, 1962 Mr. Universe

The 1947 Mr. America's contest, hosted by the Chicago Amateur Athletic Union (C.A.A.U.) was being held in Chicago on June 26th. Just three days prior Steve flew into Orchard Field Airport where he was met by Richard Trusdale. A month earlier, Richard had written to Steve and introduced himself as Alan Stephan's manager. He described how he had advanced Alan's career after the he had won the 1946 Mr. America contest, and offered to do the same for Steve.

When Reeves arrived into Chicago, Trusdale and his family were there to pick him up and graciously offer him dinner and a place to stay there at their home. Trusdale's itinerary schedule for Reeves included hiring several physique photographers within the sport, so that Steve would have his first talent portfolio put together. The images would also serve as an inventory to an eventual mail order business for him, named *The Steve Reeves Company*. The following three photographers within the field were booked; Tony Lanza from Toronto, Canada, Chicago's Paul-Stone Raymor, and Russ Warner, a California Bay Area photographer who had already taken shots of Steve several times since he was seventeen.

Trusdale, made arrangements with Lanza to photograph Steve prior to the Mr. America, and had also gave him a room at his house during his three-day stay. Lanza had first established himself as a physique photographer in 1943 for world renowned fitness entrepreneur's Joe & Ben Weider. The legendary brothers began their global empire with their first publication *Your Physique* based out of Montreal, eventually publishing most notably *Muscle & Fitness, Flex, Men's Fitness* and *Shape* magazines, along with Weider nutritional products, apparel and fitness equipment.

By the time Reeves got to Trusdale's home, Lanza was already there. Tony recalls his first impressions of Reeves. *"I remember the weather was very hot on that trip to Chicago, and my stay there at the Trusdale's."* recalls Lanza. *"When Richard and Steve arrived at the house I was in the kitchen reading the newspaper. The back door opened, and Richard walked in saying, 'Tony, I would like you to meet Steve Reeves from California.' I remember Steve was wearing this short-sleeved shirt that gave him this Lil Abner look, and he had this incredible tan, and styled hair. He looked awesome! And his shoulders, Wow! He was everything I had heard about, and then some."* The next day, Steve had his first pre-contest shoot with photographer Paul-Stone Raymor. By all accounts, it was a successful session and the somewhat half, strikingly nude stills became some of the classic shots of all time of Reeves, and incidentally predated by decades the famed *Cosmopolitan* centerfold of Burt Reynolds. Lanza, later said of the Raymor photos, *"Steve looked better than any movie star I had ever seen in those shots."*

In between scheduled photo shoots, Reeves continued to train daily. He primarily lifted at the Lawson YMCA in downtown, but also enjoyed visiting several of the other city gyms such as the popular *Billy Hill Studio*. Steve liked seeing what every facility had to offer, as some day Reeves hoped of owning his own gym, and with this in mind made continual note of each one he visited.

Much of the time that week Steve spent swimming and sunbathing at the Evanston beaches outside Chicago. Nights, he practiced his posing routine, aiming for perfection. Days later this focus would pay off. Those who saw him on the platform say he was poetry in motion.

Meanwhile, Lanza continued to scout for shooting locations, finally settling on a lake shore beach near a scenic highway. That day, Tony experienced the amazing Reeves charisma he had heard about. Steve's signature magnetic presence was a quality that everyone who met him for the first time remarked on. Even photographer Russ Warner once said, *"Steve's presence was as if he were from outer space or something!"*

Lanza, a former pro wrestler remembers that day, *"Steve was beginning to really attract a crowd while we were just walking along the sand! Even though I myself was in fairly good shape, I looked really bad beside him. I had to put back on my T-shirt so as to cover myself up! So there we were, with all these admirers walking along with us, when all of a sudden we hear this great big crash from a car accident just ahead of us. Moments later the driver involved in the wreck came up running up to us all and said to Steve, 'sir, I just caused an accident over there, and had to come over and shake your hand because you were the cause of it. I just couldn't believe my eyes!' Steve exerted this real magnetic attraction, almost as if he hypnotized people,"* said Lanza. *"I have never in all my life experience or seen anything like it."*

A series of still images of Reeves taken by Tony Lanza along Lake Michigan, 1947. Courtesy Tony Lanza

The day of the Mr. America the temperature reached balmy ninety-five degrees. The Lane Tech auditorium was jammed with fans, celebrities, reporters and photographers including a team from the International Universal Newsreel sent to cover the event. *Strength & Health* reporter Gordon Venables wrote, *"...Nothing short of a sardine could wedge their way into the pack of photographers"* assigned to the show.

Now, in the ninth year of the contest this particular event was the most lavish to date. The field of 48 contestants was the largest ever, a number sharply reduced before the first pose was struck when a dozen of the contestants looked over the competition and withdrew.

As the judges watched from a platform constructed over the orchestra pit, one by one the competitors walked out from the wings, hopped up on the main platform and struck three poses; a front, side and back pose, each lasting about ten seconds. Following each bodybuilder's moment on stage when all thirty-six men had competed, the ten judges independently tallied their scores, and then announced the individual awards.

Joe Lauriano from Honolulu, Hawaii won best abdominals. John Farbotnik won best chest. Steve Reeves won best back, but when best legs award was announced, Steve looked down and flexed his thighs and calves, believing his legs were more outstanding then his arms or back, but when they called out Kimon Voyage's name (whose legs compared to today's Pro Tom Platz) Steve felt a bit embarrassed.

Reeves' rival Eric Pedersen, representing Bert Goodrich's gym, won most muscular man award, besting Steve by just one point for the title, setting up a dramatic showdown which was to follow within minutes.

Now that the preliminary titles were announced, the leading ten bodybuilders were called out from the field of thirty-six. The top five were then asked to step forward for the awarding of the the individual trophies.

Quickly the judges announced the fifth-place winner to George Eiferman. Farbotnik of Philadelphia copped forth and Lauriano who was 1945's Jr. Mr. America took third. By now the excitement had built to a high point. A whispered undercurrent ran throughout the auditorium making it so difficult to hear that the announcer had to call for quiet more than once. During the atmosphere of suspense, the judges finally announced their decision. Suddenly the hushed auditorium heard that there was a tie for first. Steve Reeves and Eric Pedersen had each been awarded 72 points.

To decide upon the tie, a second pose down was announced. Reeves and Pedersen would again each take the platform for a separate set of three poses. Pedersen went first. The nineteen-year old blond bodybuilder struck his routine, statuesque beneath the overhead lighting, the crowd went wild. Many thought the title was his. Then Reeves took the platform. From the minute he struck his first pose, it was clear Steve had not traveled to Chicago to take second place. He flowed from pose to pose, front to back, side to side, turning his bronzed body in a choreographed cat-like fashion that emphasized speed and grace. The huge Lane Tech auditorium was eerily quiet, and then all of a sudden, a thunderous applause broke out giving way to cheers and whistles. *"I've never seen anything like it!"* said one spectator. *"I can't believe it!"* said another.

After a speedy tabulation the judges' decision was handed to the announcer, who proclaimed Steve Reeves of Oakland, California that years 1947 Mr. America, the youngest ever to achieve the professional title.

Reeves would make the cover of hundreds of magazines throughout his career, this one being his first. Courtesy Joe Sciambra

With his good looks, appealing charm and the new title, Reeves was the new star in the bodybuilding world. Reporters covering the event were quick to jump on the bandwagon. That summer Gordon Venables for *Strength & Health* wrote, *"You have to see this young man to really appreciate his build and good looks. Photos do not do him justice. He's twice as good as his pictures! It would be utter futility for me to try to describe in mere words his physique - such breadth of shoulders and narrowness of waist. His thighs and calf muscles are out of this world."*

Gene Jantzen, another competitor at the event who placed sixteenth, wrote in *Muscle Power* magazine, *"I doubt that there was one man in the contest who did not believe that Reeves would win. The West Coast has produced a lot of terrific physiques, but this one-man Reeves is the most striking example so far. He is the most perfect personification of what weight training can do that we have seen in many a day."*

Reeve's pictures appeared in every bodybuilding journal in the world and even broke into the mainstream in both *LIFE* and *LOOK* magazine. His measurements were as well-known as Betty Grable's; height 6' 1", chest 52 inches, neck 18.5", biceps 18.5 inches, calves 18.5 inches, waist 29 inches, and weight 215 pounds.

Another audience member that night saw immediate dollar signs in Reeves. When talent scout Wallace Downey first saw Reeves up on the platform, he knew immediately that this guy had the potential to become an actor or model. After the show Downey sent a letter backstage that read, '*The Wallace Downey Agency is interested in speaking with you about your possibilities in talent business, and in acting. If interested please contact me at the following telephone number, sincerely Wallace Downey.*'

The scene backstage was as frenzied as the auditorium had been in the final moments of the contest. Reporters and photographers elbowed each other for room near the new Mr. America, and jockeying for position were the International Universal Newsreel camera men.

One of those reporters covering the show for *LIFE* magazine resulted in an article that would prove to be such a bad experience for Reeves, that for the rest of his life he would later become so overly cautious with reporters that many times he opted not to speak with them.

Steve told the interviewer about his training regime and commented that body building had been very good to him. In his answer to the reporter's question about what Steve planned to do now that he had won Mr. America, Reeves responded, *"I plan to go on with college, and further my education."* Unfortunately, when the article appeared the reporter altered the quote to read, *"When my muscles stop expanding in a couple of years, I will start expanding my brain."* The betrayal stung, but Steve was particularly angry at how *LIFE* magazine twisted his words around because he knew the quote would only perpetuate the stereotype of bodybuilders as empty headed.

After the interview appeared Steve received letters from angry gym owners all over the country. His friend Bob Weidlich remembers, *"They were really pissed off at Steve for making it sound like bodybuilders were airheads, and only had muscles and no brains. They felt it hurt their gym business in attracting new members. Steve got really burned early on in publicity with that one, and I don't blame him for being upset."*

But that night when he was crowned Mr. America, nothing brought down Reeves' excitement and pride within himself. Everyone celebrated at the customary post contest dinner. Later,

Gene Jantzen and his wife offered to take Steve and Lanza back to The Trusdale's home. *"I remember that night very well,"* recalls Lanza. *"Gene's car was a small coupe that seated two, but no problem they just opened the back-rumble seat. Steve and I laughed and piled into it with Steve carrying his new Mr. America trophy. Suddenly it started to rain. We all just started laughing more. I wish I had a picture of that moment. Steve was invariably good natured and said, 'Mr. America is starting off real good for me. First, I win the show and now I'm sitting in a car trunk in the rain!'"*

A day later while waiting to leave Chicago, Steve received a call from brothers Joe and Ben Weider. They wanted to know if he would be interested in flying up to Montreal with Lanza to guest pose at their 1947 Mr. Canada show for $500.00 cash, plus expenses for the event. Reeves quickly took the offer.

"When we went up to Montreal, I showed Steve the entire city," recalls Lanza. *"He not only attracted people, but literally stopped the traffic wherever we went, especially when we hit the downtown area. The people of Montreal had never seen anything like Steve Reeves."* The contest was held at the Monument National Theatre, and the place was filled to capacity, with hundreds of people being turned away. *"To this day it was one of the best performances ever seen at the Monument National,"* remembers Lanza.

Back in Chicago, Reeves was scheduled for several radio talk shows, one being ABC's *Ladies Be Seated*, as well as other guest appearances and publicity gigs, including an appearance with Hildegarde, a popular female performer of the day.

With interviews finally over, Reeves flew back to Oakland. Goldie thrilled by his victory, waited to greet her son and, on catching sight of his Mr. America trophy, was unable to hold back a grin. Earl on the other hand was not so impressed. He still felt body building was a waste of time and that his step-son should be working in the field full time or getting an education. The relationship between Steve and Earl had always been distant and with the new title matters did not change.

"My mother backed me all the way." says Steve. *"She thought the career was a good choice, because although my father was not a bodybuilder, he was built like one. On the other hand, my stepdad Earl thought I should be out in the back yard digging holes instead of lifting weights and competing. He did not understand why a person would want to go out there and lift weights and tire themselves out when instead they could be doing something else that was more constructive."* Even though Steve was only twenty-one he had now brought home three titles, including Mr. America in just under a seven-month span. Earl still couldn't make sense of it and saw bodybuilding as a waste of time.

Over the next few days Reeves found himself thinking about the talent agency note he was given backstage in Chicago, and the opportunity of getting into acting.

On impulse Steve phoned The Wallace Downey Agency. The call got through within seconds. Reeves was now speaking to an enthusiastic Downey. The agent outlined a plan for Reeves to fly out to New York. He offered to get Steve into acting school there in Manhattan and would arrange to get an apartment for him during his stay.

The decision to quit chiropractic college was not easy but Steve felt he needed to take advantage of the opportunity in New York. After discussing the matter with both Goldie and Earl, Steve also consulted with his mentor and friend Ed Yarick, upon finally going for it. In late summer, Reeves headed east. Destination - New York City.

Steve shopping for new outfits in New York city, fall 1947. Courtesy Tony Lanza

CHAPTER SEVEN

New York

"You see that photo over there? That's my man for Samson and Delilah."

- Cecil B. DeMille, Hollywood Director, 1947

The time immediately following his 1947 Mr. America title was bittersweet for Reeves. He would seem to get a break only to encounter setbacks. *"I just couldn't win for losing,"* he said. *"Everywhere I went, they told me I was wrong."*

Motivated by Downey's enthusiasm, Steve still had high hopes for a theatrical career. On September 22, 1947 Reeves United Flight Airline landed at La Guardia. The Agency had already set their publicity machinery into action. Photographers were on hand to record the arrival of the Mr. America as he landed in New York to begin a career in show business. Knowing the public's appetite for stardom, Downey had also arranged for blond actress Jane Kean, another agency client to be in attendance so cameras could get a shot of Reeves sweeping her off her feet. The apartment leased for Steve was on East 57th. Street, a typical one-room New York city flat. It had recently been vacated by a previous tenant, a young emerging actor by the name of James Garner, who was heading to Hollywood now with film contract in hand.

Acting classes began immediately. Steve was signed up with *The Stella Adler Dramatic School for Acting* located on 42nd Street, a highly reputable school, one of which Marlon Brando had studied there four years earlier when it was called *The Dramatic Workshop Of The New School For Social Research*. Although Reeves had no training in acting, his social appearances before large scale audiences at bodybuilding shows had given him the self-confidence he needed to prove himself there. Steve was very confident he could master a stage career. He brought to this new field of study the same will, enthusiasm and determination as he had with bodybuilding. His strikingly good looks and Mr. America physique were his strengths, and he saw himself as a leading man type, a view shared by his Downey his agent. Unfortunately, Stella Adler had another agenda, one that would soon bring the two of them into conflict.

"In the beginning, Adler had us doing little skits, different scenes from different plays, as I expected," Reeves recalls. *"But then she had us talk with a lisp, or stutter, or walk pigeon toed during the performances."* When Reeves demonstrated his pigeon-toed walk, he was chastised by the Adler who pointed out that he was not performing the walk correctly. While the rest of the class looked on in amazement, Reeves confronted the formidable Adler. *"Miss Adler,"* I said, *"As a child, for ten years I had to teach myself not to be pigeon-toed, and now you tell me I don't know how to walk pigeon-toed!"* After class, Adler told Reeves he was disrupting her class, a situation she would not tolerate. She offered

to give Reeves back his money, and Steve happily accepted. *"I really wanted different training,"* he said, *"Something to prepare me for a leading man's role instead."*

The Theodore Urban School of The Theatre For Acting was just a few blocks down on 42nd. So this was Steve's second plan for acting class. Right from the start Reeves found Urban's school fulfilled his needs and expectations. Rather than being limited to acting exercises the students actually performed in plays, taking on everything from Shakespeare to modern dramas. At times, students were encouraged to improvise and to make up scenes that went along with previously produced scripts. The structure of the class worked for Steve, inspiring him in a way Adler's had not. Sword fencing was an important part of the training, and one he took to eagerly. (Roughly fifteen years later this time-honored skill would ironically serve him well when starring in such films as *Morgan The Pirate* and *The Thief of Baghdad*.) While still in school, Reeves landed his first acting job. Weekends Steve and fellow actor Dick Burney performed a comedy act which was booked within the Vaudeville circuit performing in comedy houses throughout New York, New Jersey and Pennsylvania. Although the pay was minimal, Steve was experiencing actual acting experience, performing in front of a live audience, rather than just his acting class of twenty students. Their performance was similar to that of *Martin & Lewis,* a skit about a strong man, and a skinny pal who were always arguing, but in a style similar to that of *Laurel & Hardy*. The act ran approximately 10 minutes, and they would perform roughly six skits per show. With each performance, Steve became more at ease and discovered that he really did enjoy being up on onstage, in front of hundreds of people, making them laugh. The confidence and self-esteem Steve had found through bodybuilding were continually being enhanced.

Occasionally, a fellow student from his school would attend Steve's performance. Eighteen-year old Anita Sockle, who later went under the Hollywood name of Nita Talbert was a pretty, blue-eyed blond, and former model that Steve began to date. Anita shared many of the same interests with Reeves from health and fitness, visiting museums, and simply sharing time together talking about life with one another. The courtship was brief though, as Steve's focus was more on his career, than a long-term relationship.

Anita Sockle (Steve's girlfriend) Steve, Joe Weider and Joe's then girlfriend in New York city, 1947. Courtesy Tony Lanza

Reeves was also making other contacts now in the big city, one of which was Sigmund Klein. Anyone involved within field of bodybuilding and fitness knew of Sig Klein. His gym was located at East 42nd, and 7th. and was originally owned and operated by Louis Attila, the most famous for instructing Freidrich Muller, the grandfather of body building better known as Sandow The Great. Although Attila died before Klein could ever meet him, Sigmund met and married Attila's daughter Grace, and in 1927 took over the business.

For more than a year, Klein had been reading articles about Reeves and his recent triumphs within the body building circuit. When Sig learned that Reeves was living in New York and attending acting school, Klein began calling around attempting to locate Reeves so as to invite him to join his gym. But before Sig could locate Reeves, Steve was at his front door, eager to begin weight training once again.

Klein's gym had everything to offer and was located on the second floor overlooking the theatre district. It was the best of the best in the city, and had many new innovations, one of which was the first juice bar in Manhattan. Every day, Sigmund had fresh fruit delivered to the gym, and using both a blender and a juicer would make the freshest, and nutritious sports drinks for his clients, including one that became a favorite of Reeves, a blend of carrot juice and coconut milk. *"It was great,"* recalls Reeves. *We really made some crazy recipes back then."*

The gym's environment was a very inspiring place to work out within. Over the years, Klein had collected priceless equipment and memorabilia, including everything from old kettle bells named for their unique cannon-ball shape design, to racks of chromed-plated weights, an unusual luxury for the time. The stage weights that Attila had once used in his strength shows were also on display as were barbells from Rolandow, and many other well-known stage strongmen of the late nineteenth and early twentieth century.

Reeves poses with female admirers for a New York newspaper at Sig Klein's gym, 1947. Courtesy Tony Lanza

Klein let Reeves work out there for free, just as long as the new Mr. America would help Sig bring in other bodybuilders and fitness enthusiasts to the gym. The arrangement worked well for

Steve and he occasionally gave weight instructions to new members. In spite of his full schedule at acting school, touring on the weekends performing shows with Burney, his love and passion for the sport of bodybuilding had not diminished. In mid fall of 47', Klein organized a Mr. New York contest, and naturally asked Steve if he would open the show by guest posing. Reeves readily agreed.

After his unfortunate start with Stella Adler, things seemed to be going well with Reeves' acting career. He was gaining stage experience with Burney, mastering classes at the school, and had every reason to believe that he would be as successful in theatre as he had been in professional bodybuilding. One night, in late December while performing at a movie house in New Jersey, Reeves was spotted by a Hollywood talent scout who had been sent to New York by Cecil B. DeMille. The noted producer and director was beginning to cast his latest movie spectacular *Samson And Delilah*, the biblical story about a strongman who falls for a Philistine temptress, and DeMille was searching for an actor who possessed the muscular characteristics and good looks he envisioned for the lead role.

For several months, DeMille had been sending out talent scouts up and down the West Coast to look for the ideal Samson, and although neither DeMille nor his assistants had ever seen Reeves, the bodybuilder's name repeatedly came up as an ideal candidate.

On hearing that Steve was currently attending theatre school in New York, DeMille flew an assistant out to New York to interview Reeves. At first glance, the agent was impressed, Reeves certainly had the physique and looks of a Samson, but a stage actor's presence did not necessarily translate well to the screen. The following day the scout approached *The Downey Agency* and asked if Reeves would perform a filmed screen test at the

Paramount Studios division in New York. The test film was strong enough to impress the scout, and he immediately shipped it off to DeMille.

Reviewing Cecil B. DeMille's contract are Sig Klein on the left, Steve and DeMille's talent agent at a New York restaurant, 1947. Courtesy Steve Reeves

One week later, Steve learned that DeMille wanted him for the part of Samson. He started packing his bags and made arrangements to head back West, this time to Hollywood. With the prospect of a seven-year contract, Reeves left New York on January 20th, 1948 just one day before his 22nd birthday.

Six months prior, he had arrived in Manhattan as an untrained and aspiring actor. Once again, in what has become a lifelong pattern, Reeves had not only set a goal for himself, but exceeded it. His objective at becoming a leading man in Hollywood, the very same goal that had gotten him removed from *The Stella Adler School* was now becoming a reality. With his first contract in hand, Steve now just secured a role in film by one of Hollywood's most famous producers. Success seemed guaranteed. But in another parallel pattern of his life, he would be tested by setbacks.

Nine years earlier, Judy Garland had taken the country by storm in the 1940 *The Wizard of Oz,* a tale of a mid-western girl transported to the land of Oz. Reeves must have felt the same sense of upheaval when he landed in Los Angeles on January 20th and was chauffeured to Paramount Studios.

It was only a month ago that Steve had been living in a Manhattan flat getting by on a meager salary he had earned from his weekend acts, along with and G.I. Benefits, when all of a sudden, he found himself strolling into Paramount Studios in downtown Burbank to sign a seven-year contract. Hollywood, and the Land of Oz.

The first thing Reeves noticed when he entered DeMille's office was a grouping of portraits of the Studios current stars: Dorothy Lamour, Bing Crosby, and Bob Hope. But more so Steve was utterly amazed to see in the midst of this arrangement of stars was a photo of himself, a framed photo that Tony Lanza had taken in Chicago just before the 1947 Mr. America contest, the portrait known as *Perfection in the Clouds*. In it Reeves faces the camera, arms raised high in a gesture of victory, aspiring with power, the vision of a demigod.

DeMille shook Reeves's hand and then turned and pointed to the photo saying, *'You see that man over there?'* he said to Steve, *'That's my man for Samson And Delilah!'*

Before Reeves could react, DeMille delivered his condition. He told Reeves to take a seat and bluntly informed Steve of the following. *'As you know the camera adds a good fifteen pounds to a person's body. Therefore Steve, you have to lose at least fifteen pounds, so you won't appear to heavy on screen. We need you to look just as you do in that picture up on the wall.'*

Without a moment of hesitation Steve agreed to lose the fifteen pounds, promising to go from 210 to 195.

The star treatment commenced immediately. Reeves was the newest property in DeMille's stable of stars and created a stir wherever he went. DeMille would join Steve for lunch at Paramount's commissary. He was given his own room on the lot as well as an acting coach with whom he worked with for two hours a day. Twice a month he received a hefty pay check per the conditions of his stock players contract. Starlets constantly looked for Reeves now, hoping to meet and become his girlfriend.

By now, DeMille had selected his Delilah, MGM's starlet Hedy Lamarr. Lamarr had starred in *Lady of The Tropics* in 1939, and in *Tortilla Flat* in 1942 with Spencer Tracy, and her most recent movie was *Dishonored Lady*. DeMille was convinced the sultry brunette would pair well with Reeves.

Things were going well on set, but as dress rehearsals began Reeves struggled with another problem. As promised to DeMille, he had begun to lose weight and had in fact already lost ten pounds to date. Studio executives were pleased, but when Steve visited local beaches and gyms, he received a different reaction. Fans and fellow body builders thought the weight loss was a mistake. Again, and again he would hear that he had been the greatest Mr. America ever, but with his recent drop in body weight he was not the Mr. America they all knew Reeves to look like. *'be your original self,'* he would constantly hear now from his friends. *'don't ruin your body for movie stardom.'* Meanwhile, at the studio, Reeves was beginning to feel the tension and disapproval towards him now. Shooting was to begin in three months and DeMille wanted the fifteen pounds off now!

On the lot he would hear 'lose weight!' At the gym he heard, *'you're losing your physique, and everything you have worked for!'* Everywhere he went, he felt wrong. Additionally, an inner voice warned him about the weight loss. As a teenager he had rapidly gone from 163 pounds to 193, but the last twenty pounds, the weight that he felt really accented his body and gave him the final great weight, had been hard to gain. Each pound was hard won. Now to lose it! The twenty-two year old felt as if the foundation he had built and trusted was being undermined.

The stakes for *Samson And Delilah* were high. It was to be DeMille's biggest production to date, though eventually being outstripped by *The Ten Commandments,* and the first multi-million- dollar production in Hollywood since *Gone With The Wind.* Hearing that Reeves hadn't lost the fifteen pounds, the DeMille called Reeves into his office. Cecil told Reeves that he enjoyed working with him so far, and that his acting had improved, but a bombshell was about to be dropped. Apologetically, DeMille told Reeves that the expensive production was far too great a risk and that he could not take the chance on Steve for not losing the weight.

In the self-published photo booklet, *Steve Reeves: A Tribute*, Milton T. Moore, Jr. relates the scene in which DeMille releases Reeves. *'Some days you do a very fine scene, some days you do an unsatisfactory scene,' the director said. 'Filming begins in three months and you still have not lost the weight I requested.' Then DeMille told Reeves that he was going to use Victor Mature, a veteran of seventeen films and box office draw. 'Victor is not who we want here at Paramount, he is not our ideal, physically. You, Steve in that picture on my wall, are what we want. But Samson And Delilah is going to be the first multi-million-dollar film production since Gone With The Wind, and I simply can not take a chance with you under the circumstances.'* He released Steve from his contract paying him for his work to date.

Years later Reeves recalled, *"I didn't try to explain my problem. I thanked DeMille for the opportunity. But if I had been more mature and put my values where they belonged at that time, my movie career might have started ten years earlier"*(Note: Cecil B. DeMille died in 1959 six months before *Hercules* was released in the United States, leaving forever the unanswered question of whether he would have been so quick to release Steve of his contract, had he seen Reeves up on the screen in his signature role as Hercules.)

This paradox of being admired for his looks and then finding out that his strength was a liability was to delay Reeves' entry into Hollywood. The ideal of this time was the Gary Copper or Gregory Peck types, and Reeves did not fit this type. Additionally, if casted in a picture with the idols of the time, he would physically make them look less manly. At *Universal Studios* Steve was also told by directors that he would never be contracted for a film if it were not for his muscular build. *"During those years when I was first starting out it was very stressful and discouraging,"* Reeves recalls. *"What I worked for all my life and had the most pride in was holding me back as far as being as actor."*

Faced with a dead end in Hollywood, Reeves had to reassess his goals. His decision was to move to Santa Monica beach and return to the sport of bodybuilding, an arena where he knew success, a field where there were still titles to conquer.

Steve performing a hand balancing act with female friend at Santa Monica's Muscle Beach, 1948. Courtesy Glenn Sundby, California Gymnastic Hall of Fame

CHAPTER EIGHT

Muscle Beach

"Those were the days, I'll tell you. They will never be again. It was utter freedom, total freedom. Not a worry in the world."

- Steve Reeves, 1993

Reeves moved to Santa Monica at the beginning of March 1948 and shortly thereafter Vic Tanny approached him with prospect of his competing in the upcoming 1948 Mr. USA contest, an event that would be the forerunner of today's big sponsored professional shows.

In the late 1940s, and early 50's Tanny along with business partner Bert Goodrich, staged bodybuilding events at Los Angeles famed Shrine Auditorium, shows that brought in crowds as large as six thousand. These early events were produced with classic

Hollywood pizzazz, and featured not only bodybuilders but also live bands, strength acts, tumblers and adagio dancers.

In spite of Tanny's encouragement, Reeves wasn't convinced this was the best time to compete. He had not worked out in two months and was ten pounds under his competition weight, that golden ten pounds he always felt accented his physique and gave him that winning edge. *"Steve, are you kidding me?"* said Tanny. *"You could beat anyone, just the way you are! Just work out for the next two weeks, like always and you'll look great."*

Against his instinct, and the partially influenced prospect of the one-thousand-dollar cash prize, the largest yet awarded at a bodybuilding contest, Reeves agreed. *"I wasn't in shape,"* he recalled years later, *"but at that point I needed the money, so I agreed to compete."* Sooner than he expected, Reeves was back in The Iron Game.

Two weeks later on March 13th, a five-thousand plus crowd showed up at the Los Angeles Shrine Auditorium to cheer for their favorite Mr. America as he again competed, but this time the winning physique, and grace that a year before had earned Reeves his title was absent that night. Steve was under 210 pounds, out of condition, and terribly sun burned, so burned that each motion caused him excruciating pain. In a hurried attempt to prepare for the contest he had over used a home-made sunlamp.

"I had not been out in the sun for months and burned myself so badly I could hardly move, let alone train," recalls Steve. *"The night of the contest I used make-up to cover up the blotchy sunburn areas. With the combination of lost weight, awkward posing and the make-up that concealed the definition I had, man, I didn't have a chance."* The disappointed crowd saw him lose to Clancy Ross, competitor slightly shorter and weighing roughly 200

pounds, who had previously won the 1945 Mr. America. That Saturday night, Ross was bronzed to perfection, looked flawless as he posed gracefully to the music provided by the live 20-piece orchestra.

Reeves, in spite of his sun burn and weight loss placed second, beating 1946 Mr. America Alan Stephan, one of the toughest competitors of the day. Of the competition, Reeves said, *"Clarence Ross won and should have."*

Reeves's pride took another blow that night. The contest promoters, Vic Tanny and Bert Goodrich had arranged for the winner to be given a screen test with Paramount Studios. Ironically, the test was for the role in Cecil B. DeMille's *Samson And Delilah*, the film he had just been released from the month before. Goodrich, had contacts all throughout Hollywood since his gym was located within blocks of the studios, and many of the movie stars trained with him. One such star was tenor Mario Lanza who had just finished his film debut in *That Midnight Kiss* co-starring Kathryn Grayson.

Following the loss, Reeves rededicated himself to bodybuilding. As a working and living environment, Muscle Beach proved the ideal place for this. The beach on Santa Monica was later referred to as Camelot, Brigadoom, and The Little Kingdom that disappeared. It had an ideal climate and beautiful shoreline that was the epicenter of the bodybuilding community, attracting elite lifters, gymnasts, and world class athletes as well as ardent spectators. The annual Mr. and Miss Muscle Beach contests drew worldwide attention and were covered by International News Services.

On weekend mornings hundreds of people would gather at the life guard stands next to the pier to watch the performers. On any given day, bodybuilders such as Jack LaLanne, Armand

Tanny, George Eiferman, and Joe Gold (who years later founded the worldwide franchise *Golds & World Gyms*) were there competing and posing against another.

The 1948 Mr USA line-up; 3rd place Alan Stephan, 2nd place Reeves and 1st place winner Clancy Ross. Courtesy Joe Roark

When famous entertainer and sex symbol Mae West wanted to hand pick the male members of her Las Vegas review she went directly to Muscle Beach to find them.

When the night time arrived at Santa Monica's beachfront the carnival turned absolutely elegant. The women would change from their old fashioned, thick cut bikinis into elegant dancing dresses and gowns, and the men would be transformed from hand balancers and weight lifters into zoot suit, big band swingers. For hours on end, the people of Santa Monica would dance to the big bands at the ballroom pier.

The word quickly got in the community that Reeves was now living in Santa Monica and competing on the circuit while training at Vic Tanny's gym.

At the time, Tanny's was on 4th and Broadway and was the place for die-hard body builders to lift at. Tanny ran it with his brother Armand who was 1941 Mr. Pacific Coast weight-lifting champion and later won the 1950 Mr. USA title.

Tanny, born and raised in New York City and was a well-known and respected physical culturist within the field. In 1945, at twenty-five Vic opened his first gym in Rochester, New York that would eventually grow into an empire of eighty-four gyms in total spreading across the country, reportedly landing Tanny an astounding fifteen million a year.

Vic helped Steve find a place to live when he first moved to Santa Monica after his release from Paramount. Tanny's mother, a seamstress had a shop at 160 Hill Street with a one room apartment upstairs. It was not what Steve had in mind, but it would do considering the rent was inexpensive.

Reeves's only source of income at this time was through his government G.I. payment plan called the 52-20 for newly discharged veterans. It entitled unemployed veterans to apply for a 52-week payment of $20.00 a week. During those years it was enough for him to live on until he found a steady job.

Another unemployed and footloose bodybuilder who had recently arrived in Santa Monica was George 'Pecs' Eiferman, a former Mr. Philadelphia and 1948 Mr. America who Reeves met in Chicago at last year's Mr. America. Like Reeves, Eiferman was a veteran of World War II. Born in Pennsylvania, son of immigrants he had grown up in a rough neighborhood and at the age of 13 began boxing at a gym where eventually he was introduced to weights.

During the Chicago event, Eiferman and Reeves had developed an instant bond, and formed an indestructible friendship. Although the 5'7" Eiferman was a year older that Reeves, George had the 'happy go lucky' persona that made him seem a few years younger. Their personalities were different in many ways, but Eiferman was like the brother Reeves never had.

Eiferman moved from the East coast to further his bodybuilding career, mainly on the recommendation of Steve who had told him that California had so much to offer bodybuilders, and that the opportunities and chances for success were much greater here on the West coast.

When Eiferman arrived in Los Angeles and started looking for a place to live, he contacted Armand Tanny and Joe Gold as well, two in the sport who were known to help newcomers to the area.

Armand's brother Victor offered George a place to stay, but there was a catch - it was at the gym.

A typical weekend day in 1948 at Santa Monica's Muscle beach. Courtesy Glenn Sundby, California Gymnastic Hall of Fame

Years later, Eiferman described Tanny's building where the gym was located. The second floor was an old USO and had a real American flair and warmth to it. On the walls there were huge painted murals of soldiers returning from the war, celebratory backdrops for dances that were held there for hundreds of G.I.'s and their dates. But the first floor was where it all happened, a gym that turned out many of the great champions of the day.

Coined *the dungeon,* the space was dark and damp with minimal equipment, bare wooden floors, no heat and high vaulted ceilings. But the eye-catching fixture was the enormous trampoline in the center used by gymnasts for practicing their acrobatics and routines. For the first couple of days this was Eiferman's bed. *"It was soft enough,"* jokes Eiferman, *"but if I rolled over, I'd bounce around for half an hour!"*

When Reeves found out that Eiferman was sleeping at the gym, he offered to let him sleep on the living room couch at his Hill Street apartment. Within a month they soon began looking for a larger place that they would both share the rent, one hopefully closer to the beach. Within days Reeves spotted a classified ad that read: Rooms for Rent. Looking for tenants who don't smoke and are health conscious. Write to Joy Crettaz, *Muscle House By The Sea*, Santa Monica, California.

Muscle House By The Sea could not have suited them any better. The large modern home ironically was designed and built by the famed California architect Richard Neutra and was located just one block from the ocean. The price was one dollar per night, the place was perfect.

Joy Crettaz was a seventy-year old widow who ran the boarding house for young people, and available primarily to those who were interested in health and fitness. Crettaz herself was extremely health conscious and got up every morning at five-thirty to swim in the Pacific. Years later she recalled saying of the young Reeves. *"Steve had tremendous will power and determination and should an example to all those who try to reach stardom."* she is quoted in Milton T. Moore, Jr's photo booklet *Steve Reeves: A Tribute*, *"Steve knew only work. He was a great help and inspiration and was so sought after that newcomers at the house were willing to sleep on the floor just for the honor of living in the same house with him."*

The house was perfect for Reeves and Eiferman who continued to work out and spend time with many of the other female tenants. Eiferman remembers what Reeves was like as a roommate, *"Steve was very interesting. He was very tidy, and organized, but especially neat about organizing things. My friendship with Steve over all these years has mainly been because we both admire each other's achievements. A sort of natural friendship, free flowing if you may. We both enjoyed each other's families,"* George says.

During the two years that Reeves and Eiferman trained together they developed a reputation as practical jokers. They found themselves taking part in many pranks, including one trick they used to land dates with women. While at the beach they would search for a car full of good looking ladies looking to park their vehicle for the day. They would wait until they left the car and then walk over and let the air out of a tire. At the end of the day when the women would return the pranksters would walk up and offer their assistance. Nine times out of ten the two of them would end up with a date.

When it came down to the dating scene Steve was not a collector like so many of the other guys back then. He would date one lady he really liked and stay with her. Unlike some of the other lotharios back then, like Armand Tanny and Joe Gold just to name a few.

On April fool's day Reeves remembers a joke he and the others played on a fellow lifter friend, *"We had all been hanging out at the beach waiting for our friend Bobby Higgins who also trained with us at Vic's to arrive. Bobby was this great big weightlifter from back East and had really bad eye sight and wore these thick glasses. Well, when Bobby would go to the beach he would leave his glasses at home. So, George decided to play this little trick on him and dress up like a lady and pretending to be interested in Bobby. George put this turban on, and a bikini top that coincidentally fit him quite well due to his large pectoral development. So, I went over to Bobby and convinced him that this lady over there had been staring at him all day. Before you knew it, Bobby was chasing George all over the beach thinking she was playing hard-to-get. That's how bad Bobby Higgins' eye sight was. Man, we all sat there laughing so hard while George was desperately running from Bobby, screaming for help."* Laughs Reeves.

When Steve speaks of these days he recalls idyllic times, close friendships and carefree hours. Five decades later he reminiscences about that years with detailed memory.

"The water was so crystal clear and blue, as blue as could be. I remember getting up in the morning, taking a swim in the ocean, and then having my breakfast right there on the beach." recalls Steve, *"Man, for twenty bucks a week, you could live like a king! Literally, for two dollars a day, I survived comfortably. One dollar went for rent at Joy's house, and one dollar went for food."*

For lunch, Reeves would buy a huge container of cottage cheese and mix it with nuts, raisins, and chopped fruit and bring it to the beach. *"It was great!"* he recalled. *"You'd eat half of it, and then seal it up, and save the rest for a snack later."*

Workouts at Vic's were almost identical to that of the routine Reeves established years earlier at Yarick's gym in Oakland. Steve began at nine in the morning working out for two hours straight. Mondays, Wednesdays, and Fridays he trained his whole body, beginning with shoulders, then chest, lats, biceps, and triceps. He would always finish with legs, calves and abdominal work preferring to work the body according to the way the blood flowed.

Once a week on Thursday afternoons, a group of about eight to ten guys from the gym would go out to dinner at a place called *The Round Up* near Marina Del Ray. *The Round Up* was a favorite for exhausted bodybuilders who liked the dollar-fifty buffet. *"Everything imaginable was served!"* recalls Reeves, *"From huge baked hams, sides of prime beef, enormous bowls of mashed potatoes, dozens of fruits and vegetables."* One member of the clan always irritated the management by eating three times as much as the other regular customers. *"A friend of ours,"* said Reeves, *"by the name of Malcolm Brenner never missed going to The Round Up with us. Brenner was this great big guy who loved to eat, but he sort of abused the term 'all you can eat'. He just about put The Round Up out of business."* laughs Steve. *"That's how much he could eat. It was almost grotesque. Eventually the restaurant wouldn't allow Brenner to eat on the Thursday buffets. Those were the days back then in the 1940's, I'll tell you! They will never be again. It was utter freedom, total freedom to say the least. Not a worry to think about."*

Steve sitting down after his defeat at the 1949 Mr. USA contest. Courtesy Tony Lanza

CHAPTER NINE

Still Striving For First

"I look for Reeves to be the next John Grimek of the younger generation."

-Vic Tanny, Strength & Health magazine, 1949

A new challenge soon beckoned Reeves. In 1948 the British bodybuilding organization in conjunction with Britain's primary fitness magazine *Health & Strength* put together the second Mr. Universe contest to date. The event was slated to be held in London and was being advertised as the highest award yet to be given in competitive bodybuilding.

As soon as Reeves heard about the contest, he set about planning for the trip to England, and saving for his air fare and expenses. To supplement his veteran's stipend Steve took on several part time jobs, including parking cars as a valet attendant at *The Captain's* Table, as well as fueling cars at a local gas station.

Commercial sponsorship's during these years were unheard of. *"It was not like it is today,"* Reeves recalls, *"where most bodybuilders who compete for a living have sponsors. It just was not heard of, plus no company or individual in their right mind would think to support someone in a sport that was not even considered a sport."*

The competitions back then were also completely different in one primary aspect, that being steroids were not being used yet. They did not even enter into general use until the nineteen-sixty's, although there were rumors that the Russian power lifting teams had begun experimenting with the drugs. Today, Reeves totally opposes the use of steroids within the bodybuilding community, and not just out of nostalgia for the old days, but for reasons of aesthetic purity and health concerns. In a 1993 interview with *FLEX* magazine Reeves responded to a question regarding steroids. *"I think the introduction of steroids was the worst thing to ever happen to the field of bodybuilding,"* he said. *"To me the bodybuilders of today look like clones. In other words, they all look like they're out of the same mold. Sure, some of them have blond hair, some have black hair, some have fair skin, and others dark skin, some are shorter, and some are taller, but all of them look like they were stamped out of the same mold. And that's the sort of bloated-tissue look caused by steroids. In my day, from one hundred yards away you could tell if a person was John Grimek, or Clarence Ross, or Reg Park. People were individuals at that time. Now they work out with the same routine, with the same steroids, and as a result, they have come to look too much like each other. I never heard of steroids until the mid-1960's,"* Reeves said. *"In my day, bodybuilding was a health-oriented activity instead of a drug-oriented sport."* Steroids surfaced in bodybuilding, Reeves believes because people wanted to take the easy way to get to the top. *"When one guy took the easy way and got some results, somebody else did it also, and it just snowballed from there,"* he recalls. *"Even the judges encouraged it by giving out trophies to the people with the 'largest legs', not the 'best developed' and so on. It just got out of hand. If everybody got off steroids I think the quality of physiques would improve, because all of the athletes would be competing at their ideal weight."*

Reeves arrived in London on August 10th, three days before the contest. The lengthy flight and the eight-hour time difference left him exhausted but determined to win and Reeves was not about to let his fatigue affect him.

As always, his appearance generated interest and admiration. The organizer of the contest was former Mr. Europe Oscar Heidenstam who would eventually become very influential to Reeves's career. Heidenstam was one of the many people there in attendance who were very impressed by the young Californian with the engaging personality.

Years later in a small five-page pamphlet detailing Reeves' bodybuilding career, Heidenstam fondly recalls his meeting with Steve. *"My first glimpse of Reeves was at the lifting event at the 1948 summer Olympic Games in London. Reeves arrived in the middle of this one competition and almost stopped the show. His dress by the standards of the day was 'way out.' He wore a lavender silk suit with no lapels and a silk flowered shirt. He was incredibly handsome with his flawless skin burnt to a deep tan by the California sun, flashing white teeth and a head of incredibly beautiful hair. By the end of the lifting event, Steve was besieged by women and autograph hunters who finally had him stripped to his trousers showing his amazing physique. I also remember meeting nineteen-year old Reg Park and asked Reg what he thought of Reeves and his comment was concise and to the point:*

Steve's appearance at the 1948 summer Olympic games, several days prior to the Mr. Universe contest. Courtesy Tony Lanza

'Out of this world!'" (Reg Park was later to be the main inspiration to Arnold Schwarzenegger.) Heidenstam concluded by mentioning how great Steve was to become, *"...others in their way have been equally sensational of course, and the physical culture world has stood in awe of them, men such as Grimek, Park, etc., stand supreme, but there is a special place for Steve Reeves in the archives of physical culture – perhaps it was because he was ahead of his time. People can look at pictures of Steve taken twenty-years ago, and they do not age. They could have been taken last week. I remember Reeves telling me right from the age when he first became muscle conscious at 16, that he was a big lad. He told me that he could never remember his arms under 14 inches, and by the time he was 18 his biceps were also 18 inches."*

Observers often commented on Reeves' tan, and one of the secrets of his even skin tone was related to diet. He deliberately consumed a lot of iron. *"I would eat lots of raisins,"* he says, *"and drink enormous amounts of carrot juice. The reason that I did this was that iron in your system makes your skin a little reddish, a blush color and carrot juice makes your skin color a bit orange. So red and orange together, with a little sun will give you a real brilliant tan."*

The competition was intense mainly because of John Grimek, the king of all bodybuilders who entered into the competition undefeated. The sponsors of the contest had good reason to crow. An advertisement in Britain's *Health & Strength* who was published by the prestigious Link House of London enthusiastically wrote, *"The great John Grimek has asked us to say that he is doing all he possibly can to be present at this most representative of contests and we know all our readers will give him a tremendous welcome."*

One bodybuilding enthusiast who was there that night was American soon to be pioneer fitness legend Bob Delmonteque and recalls of Reeves being a crowd favorite. *"When Steve was in London for the Mr. Universe contest in 1948 he literally stopped traffic wherever he went,"* Delmonteque wrote in Robert Kennedy's *MuscleMag International* magazine years later. *"Standing over six feet tall with dark wavy hair, and pearly white teeth, he was irresistible to the ladies. They not only liked Steve, they loved him! I remember back in the old days Steve and I went back stage at the theatre and I said, 'Steve let's run over and get us a girl,' and he said, "No Bob, we are going to walk over there and get them all!' We took all eight ladies from that chorus line with us that night!"*

The intense competition between the younger Reeves and the legendary Grimek had the crowd primed for a classic battle, and they were not disappointed. When the time came for the pose downs between the two of them Reeves went first, taking the stage to the sound of the thunderous crowd. It took several minutes for the audience to quiet down. Several women even fainted.

As he hit his poses; side lat shot, side chest, double biceps, and full back the crowd screamed and cheered making it clear to the judges that Reeves was a favorite. In what was to become his trademark style, Steve ran through his poses quickly with the entire routine lasting no more than thirty seconds. (This unconventional approach to posing was not always beneficial to Reeves and some even believe it cost him valuable points throughout his professional career.) Steve's routine ended with an unexpected note. Reported Delmonteque, *"Steve was so nervous that he lost his balance and slipped off the platform. But he got a standing ovation that lasted about five minutes."*

Years later in an *Ironman* article, John Grimek referred to the fall. *"Reeves, who was watching me at the time, I think got kind of nervous and when he walked out he wobbled in his footing. And* in one case, he missed his step and fell off the platform. I think that just put him out of the picture."

Grimek was on next and mesmerized the crowd. Delmonteque recalls, *"He did cartwheels into poses, splits into double bicep poses, handstand poses, flexing calf and thighs doing press ups (handstands). His muscle control was amazing. What a show John Grimek and Steve Reeves put on,"* he said. *"I believe this was the greatest bodybuilding show ever."*

Unable to elect an immediate winner, the judges called back Reeves and Grimek to the stage and gave them each three-minutes on the podium to perform any poses or routines they wished to.

Still the judges anguished over their decision, and then one offered this suggestion, why not give the award to the competitor who was the better gymnast?

The idea may or may not have come from Bob Hoffman, a close friend and employer of Grimek's. Right at that point, well before Grimek even completed his posing routine, Steve knew he had lost, and that the contest was over.

The decision was rendered amid the crowd's roar. Andre Drapp from France placed third, Steve Reeves placed second and John Grimek took the first place. *"I have never seen so much commotion and enthusiasm at any physique show as at this one,"* Delmonteque added *"It was truly unforgettable."*

Reeves's speech as he accepted his second-place trophy was gracious saying, *"John Carl Grimek is the greatest bodybuilder that ever lived!"*

Later Steve said of his loss to Grimek, *"No one told me in advance that I was expected to outdo Grimek in an area other than bodybuilding. I was under the impression that the Mr. Universe was a physique contest."* Looking back on the contest with good humor, Reeves says, *"All you had to do was look at the sixty-year old faces on the judge's panel to know I had no chips. Grimek was forty now, and it was a big deal in those days. The judges knew that years 1948 Mr. Universe was Grimek's last hurrah. I, on the other hand, was just twenty-two and with several more bodybuilding years ahead of me."*

Even though he was publicly gracious following his loss to Grimek, Reeves was disappointed to have placed second.

The day after the contest, Oscar Heidenstam approached Steve with news of another competition that was about to be held in Europe – The Mr. World contest being held in Cannes, France.

The 1948 Mr. Universe ceremony. Andre Drapp 3rd, Grimek 1st and Reeves 2nd.
Courtesy Joe Sciambra

Organized by the Federation Francaise de Culture Physique the event was a prestigious show. Oscar invited Reeves to join him on the trip. The idea of another contest helped take the sting out of the loss and Steve readily accepted Heidenstam's invitation.

On the train ride south, Heidenstam noticed a small wooden box Reeves carried and soon discovered another component of Steve's training regiment. *"Reeves was the first bodybuilder I ever saw using food supplements. The box was divided into several components."* Heidenstam recalled for a *Health & Strength* interview at that time. *"He had about eight different pills, from concentrated goat milk, protein, glucose, and molasses."*

Once in Cannes, they stayed at the Palm Beach Hotel overlooking the Mediterranean Sea. Reeves trained pool side during the day, occasionally taking time out to mingle and joke with the French women so eagerly to meet and talk with vibrant American.

The contest was held on Monday, August 16th. And Reeves was the only American who entered. Once again standard poses combined with gymnastic skills were aloud earning additional points from the judges. As he had done in London, Reeves settled for a straightforward presentation of poses, but this time, in spite of his lack of gymnastic ability, his extraordinary build tipped the scales in his favor and he easily outdistanced his rivals.

As Reeves was pronounced that years 1948 Mr. World champion. Steve took center stage and graciously accepted a huge floral tribute and the trophy an antique Sevres vase. Heidenstam, who placed fifth remembered Reeves asking him, *"What am I to do with this damn vase?"* laughed Steve. Oscar had to explain to him the history and value of the vase, *"I had to explain to Steve that it was probably worth around three hundred U.S dollars back then!"*

1948 Mr. World winner – Steve Reeves front and center. Courtesy Steve Reeves

Following his win, Reeves received royal treatment. It was a glorious and memorable time with lots of gourmet meals, special events and lovely ladies to celebrate with.

After the contest, Reeves returned to California. In spite of his triumphs in Europe, his situation at Santa Monica remained largely as it had before he left for the Mr. Universe competition. Although money was still tight, he remembers these times as enjoyable. Part of the fun for Reeves and his friends was devising ways to beat the system. When offered a free dinner he was quick to accept.

"When a girl asked me to stop by for a visit," Reeves says, *"I would reply by saying, only if I can stay for dinner. Then if they would say okay, which most of them did, I would get all dressed up because the majority of them still lived at home with their parents. That way I could not go wrong. I would impress her parents, and I would get a great meal out it too."*

Before the meal had ended, many parents often envisioned Reeves as a prospect for their daughter to marry. *"And that's when I knew it was time for me to say good night and thank them all for dinner,"* Steve recalls with a laugh.

The apartment Reeves shared with Eiferman was only a few blocks away from the pier in Santa Monica. *"Almost every day I would go down to the beach and sunbathe, primarily to get a tan and watch the crowds,"* Reeves remembers. *"But the beach was definitely my scene for picking up girls, and not the clubs and dancing joints. The beach is where it happened for me. By the time I had arrived at the beach, I would have five to six women sitting next to my blanket in no time. It was great."*

Reeves was never one for dancing, although he did attempt taking lessons around this time and tried his luck on the dance floor once. *"I didn't really like dancing, because, it really wasn't my thing. It was one thing posing up on stage in front of thousands of people all alone, but to be watched and critiqued at something that right from the beginning I did not do very well at, well that's another thing. So, dancing and I weren't really compatible."*

He was not one for late nights either. In fact, Steve made a point of getting to bed no later than ten o'clock every night, so that he would get at least nine hours of sleep a night. Health and training always came first. *"We were really health conscious back then, as we still are today. We were really training hard back then and required more rest and recuperation time, so we rarely stayed up late at night,"* recalls Reeves.

Steve's primary aim was to be as healthy and fit as possible. After his Mr. America win in 1947 he told a reporter, *"I plan on being the healthiest man in the world as well was one of the best built."*

He stamped the world of physical culture with his own interpretation and personality and grew to become a cult-figure and legend in his own lifetime. He was a trend setter in the arena of physical culture. Reeves was jogging in the Santa Cruz mountains in an era when anyone running by himself, let alone in the early morning was denounced as strange. Sometimes he drove out into the desert by himself and trained in the hot sun, performing sprints and other exercises to burn off fat and calories faster. He was the first physique champion to extol yogurt as an ideal beverage because of its rapid digestion. Eiferman remembers, *"Steve was the person who introduced whole yogurt to the bodybuilders at Muscle Beach. He said it was a health food containing friendly bacteria, but when I looked for them I never could find any!"* laughs Eiferman.

Steve was also among the first to own a Weber blender and conceptualized drinking breakfast before a morning workout, preferring high energy drinks that would enter the system rapidly while he exercised rather than working out on a bloated stomach. Thirty years before *Gatorade* was developed, Steve pioneered combining lemon juice, honey and water as a training drink. He took great care of his teeth, strong and cavity-free, brushing them with baking soda and salt, while massaging the gums with the same solution to keep them hard.

His individuality carried over into other areas as well. He wore custom designed tapered shirts when nobody else was wearing them and would get his hair professionally styled when men's hair shops were unknown, possessing the confidence to have the job done in women's beauty salons, the only available facilities at the time.

In the gym, Steve developed the man's physique to the limit of physical perfection. His tools were simple enough; cold, inert masses of iron.

In late September of 1948, Reeves spent some time back in Oakland visiting his mother and friend Ed Yarick. While there Steve also went to visit one of bodybuilding's top photographers, Russ Warner. Russ had been taking physique shots of Reeves since he was sixteen years old and had invited Steve to visit him again so that he could take some current photos of Steve for his portfolio. They drove to Stinson beach and the nearby hills, a site where many of the top bodybuilders of the day were photographed. The photos taken by Warner that day, along with Tony Lanza's shots alongside Lake Michigan captured the all-time classic physique of Steve Reeves.

After the shoot, Warner and Reeves returned to Oakland and met up with Jack LaLanne. *"I'll never forget that evening,"* Warner remembers. *"When Steve entered the restaurant with us, every man, woman, and child stopped eating. You could hear their knives and forks hit the table. Some of them froze with their mouths hanging open. They looked at him in amazement, as if he were a man from another world. Of course, ninety nine percent of them had never heard of Steve Reeves and thought he must have been a movie star."*

Asked what made Steve Reeves different from the scores of other bodybuilders, Warner replied, *"Genetics. Steve has the most ideal genetics for bodybuilding that I have ever seen or photographed, and I have had the occasion to work with, photographically speaking most of the top bodybuilders in the world, from Arnold Schwarzenegger, to Frank Zane and Bill Pearl. So, I have definitely been able to see and compare who I think had the best physique ever, and Reeves is still the best."* Later Russ added, *"I don't think there is one chance in 50 trillion that the particular mix of hereditary genes that produced the product we see in Steve Reeves will ever occur in combination again. Steve was a very unusual bodybuilder. He had an overall beauty that no other bodybuilder has ever been able to achieve. When the good Lord made Steve Reeves, he broke the mold. There has never been another man, as we go back through all written word and graphic representation who from head to toe, ever came out like Steve did. He's simply from another world."*

Warner, like few others had the chance to not only hang out with Reeves, but to witness some of Reeves's workouts then. Reflecting back, today Warner gives a picture of the Reeves he knew more than fifty years ago.

"Steve was a very private person, somewhat quiet and reserved, but very well liked. But when you got him in the gym, he transformed into a work of art when he worked out. He was totally phenomenal! Even though he did not work out with the heavy weights like Clancy Ross, or Alan Stephan did, Reeves still out did them all in proper style and form. He was so focused when training that many times you would wonder if he even knew other people were around him watching. Not only was Steve always working to complete projects and setting goals for himself, but he was very inquisitive. He was a scientific bodybuilder of his time and was very advanced in nutrition. His exercise program was designed specifically for himself to tailor his own physique and needs."

While still training and bodybuilding, Reeves had not given up on his dream of becoming a movie actor. Eiferman, his roommate at this time remembers one Sunday afternoon when

Reeves wanted to try and make a cowboy movie with the use of an old 16mm silent movie camera. The two of them went to Will Rogers State Park located in Beverly Hills and rented two horses. Eiferman had only ridden a few times before that, but Reeves was an expert horseman. They rode up into the hills with the camera to try and make a self-made cowboy film. After they had gotten about half way through the reel, Reeves wanted to shoot a scene of him racing his horse around this bend of a trail and directed Eiferman to capture the scene. The horses knowing that they were heading home for their food soon were somewhat edgy. Eiferman recalls, *"It was all set up. I began filming the camera in my location just before Steve made his grand appearance where he quickly rode around the bend on his horse, and I mean really moving. Then all of a sudden, Steve and his saddle kept going with the turn, while Steve's horse went the other way flying by me back for the barn where his food was. All I saw of Steve after that was in this ditch all tangled up in his saddle covered with dust and branches. I immediately dropped the camera thinking he was badly hurt. As I ran down to see if he was all right, Steve was half smiling saying, 'did you shoot it? Did you shoot it?' And all I could say was, no, I thought you were hurt so I stopped filming right after you fell off. And Steve was so furious at me. He just got up, wiped off the dust and dirt and picked up his saddle, still insisting on why I didn't keep shooting the scene. He was so mad at me for that."* Laughs George.

    The frustration of holding onto the dream of becoming an actor in the face of universal opposition remains fresh even decades later. *"From 1948, shortly after my release from Paramount and up until late 1950 was a very frustrating time for me,"* Reeves recalls. *"I was still trying very hard every month to convince certain Hollywood companies like MGM, Universal, and various other film companies that I was perfect for movies and that if they could just see past the fact that bodybuilders did not belong in Hollywood I could prove them wrong. But I was turned away constantly, so it was tough trying to persuade them to give me a shot. It was a never, ending battle."*

It is almost impossible to imagine a time when Hollywood did not want leading men with muscular builds. Today, casting directors can not get enough of muscle and brawn. Actors are encouraged to lift weights, hire trainers and build muscle so that they can take on the look of a Jean-Claude Van Damme, Sylvester Stallone and of course Arnold Schwarzenegger. This demand crosses gender lines. Demi Moore and Linda Hamilton worked with personal trainers to develop muscular physiques for body revealing roles.

But in the late forties, bodybuilding and Hollywood film making did not mix.

Still Reeves, in characteristic fashion persevered. He did not exactly know when, but he knew that he was destined to become the first bodybuilder to turn actor in Hollywood.

In the meantime, he had another competition to prepare for. At Vic's Dungeon, Steve along with Clancy Ross, Alan Stephan, Floyd Page, Armand Tanny, and George Eiferman were all training now for the approaching 1949 Mr. USA contest, a highly promoted L.A. show. It was reported that every major bodybuilder on the West coast was going to enter, among them was Reeves's rival John Grimek. Steve looked at it as a chance to come back and regain his status as the true number one champion.

On March 26th, a crowd of more than six thousand five hundred spectators filled the mammoth Shrine Auditorium in Los Angeles. Describing the scene that night Lewis Pike wrote in *Strength & Health*, *"When I went back stage to get the scoop on the contestants, half way through I noticed Reeves sat in his quiet manner over in the corner with some well-wishers. Eiferman joked with others, and Grimek swung from a pull up bar, and Ross was combing his hair."*

Like many times, Reeves remained separate, but centered. Then, once again bad luck hit. That night he was not only defeated by Grimek, but came in third, bested by Clancy Ross who took second.

It was little consolation that the audience disagreed with the judge's verdict, believing that Grimek no longer had the winning physique of his younger days.

In a 1994 interview Clancy Ross spoke of that night, *"The crowd was in a complete uproar when Grimek was declared first. I can still hear the crowd booing and hissing because they did not agree that Grimek should have won. Some said it should have been Steve, some said it should have been me, but whatever the case may be, Grimek was definitely not liked by many of the spectators that night."*

Many believed Grimek was not really all he was publicized to be, and that he lacked the symmetrical physique of a bodybuilders like Ross, Pedersen and Reeves but Grimek's win that night made him the only undefeated bodybuilder in the history of the sport.

Again, after the decision was announced, there was a swirl of controversy about the role John Grimek's friend Bob Hoffman might have played in the decision making. Hoffman had been a judge for the Miss USA contest held prior that night to the competition and was the master of ceremonies for the main event of the Mr. USA.

There has always remained a sense of speculation as to just how much influence Bob Hoffman really had on the judging, regarding his friend John Grimek.

The 1949 Mr USA line-up; 2nd place Clancy Ross, John Grimek 1st and Steve Reeves 3rd. Courtesy Clancy Ross

Because of the lasting impact Reeves has had within the field of bodybuilding, fans several generations removed from his era are often astonished to learn that Steve failed to place first in several of his competitions. Reeves placed second to Grimek in the 1948 Mr. Universe, and then second to Clancy Ross at the 1949 Mr USA contest. These losses created some of the most heated controversies within the sport of bodybuilding to date.

In the short amount of time between his win at the 47' Mr. America and the 49' Mr. USA titles, Reeves had brought a tremendous amount of positive attention and greater public interest to the sport of bodybuilding. Intelligent and conscientious, Steve was a powerful spokesman now for the sport, and the physical culture revolution.

The spring of 1949 brought Reeves many paid public guest appearances. In addition to posing, he talked about the benefits of health and fitness. One of the appearances took place in Hawaii. Steve traveled there with Eiferman and Les and Pudgy Stockton. Pudgy was one of the first great female bodybuilders of the time, as well as an accomplished hand balancer.

The group took part in two big physique shows in Honolulu to help raise money to send the Nuuanu weight lifting team back stateside for the National Weight lifting Championships. Just weeks after his appearance in Hawaii, Reeves flew to Vancover, British Columbia where he guest-posed at the 1949 Mr. British Columbia contest.

Again, he used the opportunity to promote health. When Vancover journalist Jack Richards asked him what he most cherished, Reeves replied, *"Health is the thing,"* adding, *"I expect to live to the ripe old age of 100 years, no problem!"*

In the spring of 1949 while attending a health seminar in Los Angeles Reeves was introduced to Bernarr McFadden a multi-millionaire known within the health Field as an eccentric man. At 81, Bernarr had built an empire based on a chain of fitness magazines, newspapers, several hotels and health spas. McFadden admired Reeves and offered him a full-time job as physical instructor and recreational director at his latest venture – *The Arrow Head Springs Hotel & Spa* a facility McFadden was leasing in the mountains just north of San Bernardino. *"Working for McFadden that summer was very interesting,"* recalls Steve. *"Bernarr was a real eccentric and unique individual. I remember he would wear these shoes he had specially made with steel plates on the soles so that he could absorb more positive magnetism through the earth."* For three months Reeves worked at McFadden's spa. *"Every morning I would start the day off by leading the clients, most of whom were elderly women, on nature walks, or on horseback rides through the mountains. I really enjoyed it because I was outside in the fresh air, riding horses and getting paid for it."* While the living conditions for Steve were very comfortable, a one-room cabana poolside, the agenda McFadden had in mind for him was not. McFadden wanted Reeves to act as a male escort for the older women at nights. *"Bernarr wanted me to be more than just a physical instructor,"* Reeves recalls. *"His idea was that every night I dance with these elderly women and escort them throughout the evening. That's when I drew the line."* Reeves wanted out of the job quick.

Back in Los Angeles, Bert Goodrich, asked Reeves and George Eiferman to appear as guest at all of the grand openings for his new chain of health gyms. The two-city tour started in Phoenix, Arizona where Goodrich was born and raised, and went on to Salt Lake City, Utah where the the Mr. Salt Lake City contest was being held in conjunction with the final gym opening of Goodrich's chain.

There were, at this time several press reports that Reeves had stopped working out completely, lost weight, and became susceptible to colds and depression, but these rumors were totally incorrect. Steve was healthy and fit, and although keeping a low profile after his third-place finish in the Mr. USA he continued to train as always.

In the meantime, Eiferman was developing a career as a spokesman for the National School Assemblies Agency eventually putting on fifteen to twenty shows per week, XXXepictio five hundred schools per year. Occasionally Reeves helped out by assisting Eiferman in strength feats.

Steve recalled one event with George held at Woodberry College in Los Angeles. *"About two weeks before this show, we started practicing this one routine where I was to pick George up by my teeth. So, I had to make this contraption out of leather for my teeth, and for George to hook onto. I first started out by picking up a one-hundred- pound barbell with it, then 150 pounds and when I got up to 200 pounds I knew I was ready to George who at that time was probably around 210 pounds. It was not easy, but we pulled it off, and the people loved it."* For the event Reeves wore a Li'l Abner outfit he had used for a prior appearance at a Sadie Hawkins day festival that spring. The women's wolf calls and whistles could be heard outside the auditorium.

When Eiferman looks back on those days he says, *"The main thing that makes people so interested in Reeves, even more than fifty years after his retirement from bodybuilding is that Steve is a real one of a kind"* he says. *"He achieved so much in so many areas, that people are very intrigued and fascinated. He had many fans, and his appearance was very unusual and rare. He was highly intelligent, goal oriented, enterprising and most of all an innovator. Steve was sort of a lonesome Li'l Abner, but with a real cowboy heart."* George adds, *"We really had some great times back then, and I'm glad to say I had many of them with Steve."*

Soon the roommates, and training partners would be back in the gym with a new goal in mind, another shot at the Mr. Universe title.

Reeves performing a four-hundred-pound deadlift using only his fingertips to lift the iron while training at the *York Barbell Club* prior to 1950 Mr. Universe Contest. Courtesy Steve Reeves

CHAPTER TEN

London

"The accepted opinion of the fellows in the gym was that he didn't have a chance winning Mr. Universe."

- John Grimek, York Barbell Club, 1950

By May of 1950, Reeves decided to compete once again in the 1950 Mr. Universe competition which was to be held in London the following month. *"I guess it was because I still had something to prove to myself,"* Reeves recalls. *"The Mr. Universe was the highest award given then, so it was like going for the gold."*

He knew that Eiferman was living back in Pennsylvania and training at *The York Barbell Club* while touring with his National Assembly school shows. Eiferman, one of only three training partners Reeves ever trained with during his career was an ideal trainer with whom to prepare for the contest. Even to this day, Eiferman and Reeves remain very close in friendship and speak with one another frequently.

"George was a really good training partner," Reeves remembers. *"He was a good, strong guy, and he would be there to help you out at any time if he could. I tried to be there in life to help him out as well, and I did."*

"Steve never forgot about me," Eiferman says. *"Especially years later when he made it big in Hollywood. He offered me other parts in his films and was always very generous to me."*

Back in York, the duo began focusing on the approaching Mr. Universe which due to poor organization and lack of promotion had been canceled the year before. Reeves was determined to go after the title once again.

Steve Reeves was credited for having well-shaped calves. Here he is doing a "Hack" lift in the old York gym. It was his favorite thigh exercise which also influenced his calf development.

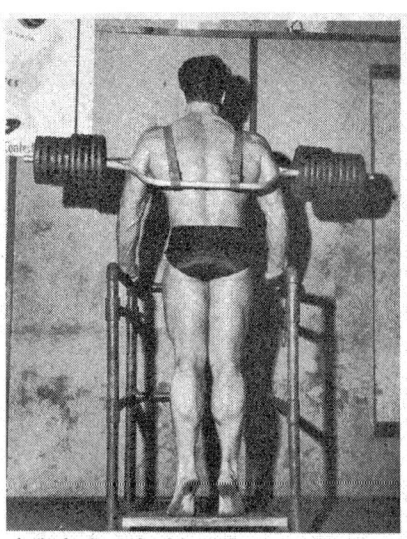

Another favorite exercise of his was the raise-up-on-toes on a high block. Here he uses a yoke with weights that fits over the shoulders and makes it easier to concentrate on working the calves without bothering to balance the weight. (York photos)

A series of York Barbell Company photos from *Strength & Health* magazine exhibit the unique training routines Reeves performed prior to the 1950 Mr. Universe. Courtesy Tony Lanza

By this time, he was powerful, and world famous, the youngest Mr. America in history, and far removed from the timid ten-year old who had immigrated as a young, fatherless boy from Montana. Now at twenty-four Steve had won or placed in seven professional physique contests; winning the Mr. Pacific twice, the Mr. America and Mr. World once, placed second in the Mr. Universe and Mr. USA contests, placed third in the 1949 USA a career statistic second only to the undefeated John Grimek.

In spite of his record, many of the muscle magazines began to write that Reeves career was over, especially after his third place showing in the 49' Mr. USA. They even reported that when Steve arrived in York to begin training for the Mr. Universe again that he was coughing and skinny.

One of those at the York Barbell Club who was keeping a close eye on Reeves was that of John Grimek, a current associate editor for *Strength & Health* magazine published by none other than Bob Hoffman. Grimek's own personal earnings were made through his own name by advertising products attached to the York Barbell Company, such as iron weights and lifting accessories. (A similar partnership would develop in the late nineteen sixties and seventies when Joe Weider used Arnold Schwarzenegger's name and photos to promote and sell his own *Weider* products in his publication *Muscle Builder).*

In a 1970 interview Grimek remembered recalled this time. *"When he (Reeves) stripped for his first workout it seemed that he had lost everything but his legs,"* Grimek said. *"The accepted opinion of the fellows in the gym was that he didn't have a chance of winning the 1950 Mr. Universe. I, too, had my doubts at that time, but we underestimated Reeves's ambition and drive."*

Within days, Reeves had gained muscular body weight and by the end of the second week showed remarkable gains. As he had while training for the Mr. America, Steve used the last names of his rivals within the sport for motivation. This time it was Britain's Reg Park's name he used to drive him on, yelling out Park's name throughout his reps.

During Reeves career, this ability to condition himself into a winning competitive state was a Steve Reeves trademark. A transformation that would have taken another bodybuilder months to achieve, Steve managed it in weeks. Witnesses swear that he seemed to grow at will. Today, of course this ability is shared by many, but in Reeves' time it was unheard of. It is a craft which requires knowing one's body and the way it reacts to exercise, nutrition and rest. It requires knowing how to generate motivation. And it requires discipline.

"Reeves didn't sit around talking, and killing time," Grimek recalls. *"Instead he went from one exercise to another. He knew the time was getting short before he would be vying for the Mr. Universe title. He put everything into his training."* The whispering in the gym, the questions about whether, or not he could win all together stopped. *"Everyone agreed it would take a damn good man to beat Steve now,"* Grimek recalled. *"If he could be beaten!"*

What others in the gym didn't know was that two weeks after he arrived in York, Reeves had contracted the flu. *"I kept training,"* he recalls, *"because I knew I needed to win that title. But when I coughed, I would almost faint."* Still he hung in there. *"I lost a bunch of fat suddenly and hardened up real quick. Ironically, the illness gave me the definition I needed quicker than usual."*

Just before he Reeves left for London, someone at the gym questioned whether or not he was as strong as he thought, a query greeted with a few snickers. When Reeves overheard the comment he simply replied, *"I can be as strong as I want to be. Follow me."*

Without another word, Steve proceeded to load a seven-foot Olympic bar with four hundred pounds of iron. He then reached down and with his arms fully extended to span more than six feet gripped the iron plates with only his fingers and promptly dead lifted the four-hundred pounds using the strength of his hands, shoulders, and legs and quickly silencing the doubting voices. Bob Hoffman was so impressed by this feat that he printed a photograph of the event taken by photographer Johnny Terpak for the August 1950 of *Strength & Health*.

Although Steve did not seek this kind of informal competition, he had previously taken on similar challenges, one of which was from Armand Tanny and George Eiferman just months before. Eiferman recalls, *"One day, Steve, Armand and I decided to have a contest to see who could clean the most weight from a kneeling position."* At the time Armand and George were regarded as two of the strongest men in the sport. *"There was no contest!"* Eiferman laughs. *"Steve beat us all by cleaning 225 pounds on his knees!"*

Despite these achievements, Reeves continually emphasized that he was working for proportion and symmetry, not brute strength. Proportion, and not the amount of weight Steve could lift was what he aimed for.

Steve's focus and dedication were frequently noted by others working out at the York gym. Reeves reflects back on this mind set as, *"You can't think about other things when you're lifting weights. This will detract from the effectiveness of the exercises and their purposes. It is really mind over matter."*

The balance he sought in his physique, he also maintained in his life. *"Don't let bodybuilding dominate your life,"* he advises years later. *"Forget about the sport when you are not in the gym. Enjoy yourself. To many people allow themselves to be a slave to their training and think muscle's 24 hours a day. If you feel like a day off, take one. You may lose some size, but you can always get it back with a few harder training sessions. Overall, you will probably feel a lot better taking that one day off that will in turn help out your other workouts."*

Today, of course Reeves trains only for health and fitness, but even when he was entering competitions he would take many days or even weeks off from heavy training to enjoy other activities in life.

On June 22nd, Steve flew from New York to London for the 1950 Mr. Universe competition. Already, in its third year now the title was now recognized as the highest award in the sport of bodybuilding. In future years its reputation would grow dramatically, drawing in competitors such as Arnold Schwarzenegger, Mickey Hargitay (husband of movie star Jayne Mansfield) and Sean Connery (James Bond 007).

Reeves was confident that he was going to take the title, but the pre-contest hype centered on Britain's favorite Reg Park. Years later, Park would become the mentor and idol for Arnold Schwarzenegger, an idol himself soon to be of a new generation several decades later.

The general opinion was that Reg Park was a sure bet to win. The promoters in London were counting on Reg's victory and donated a very rare, and valuable bronze sculpture as the first-place award, certain that it would not leave the country.

The rare sculpture was a depiction of Eugen Sandow, the father of physical culture, and was designed and forged as a limited set of only three statuettes. In 1895 Eugen Sandow commissioned sculptor Fred William Pomeroy to create and mold the trophies.

Pomeroy made the pieces for the 1901 Eugen Sandow Competition for Physical Culture held in Albert Hall, in London. The contest had over fifteen-hundred applicants, and one-hundred and fifty finalists that performed before an audience of fifteen-thousand. Sandow was one of the judges along with Sir Charles Fawes and Sir Arthur Conan Doyle British writer best known for his detective fiction featuring the character of Sherlock Holmes. Sandow himself presented the gold trophy to William Murray of Praisley, Scotland who also won Great Britain's Most Perfectly Proportioned Man. The silver statuette went to the runner-up, and the bronze to the third-place winner. It was the bronze trophy originally bestowed to Mr. A.C. Smith of London in 1901 that was now being presented to the winner of 1950 Mr. Universe.

When Steve arrived in London he was greeted by enthusiastic fans who fondly remember him from the 1948 Mr. Universe. Anticipation built daily and the contest held on June 24th did not disappoint audience members who showed up looking for a duel between the young American and United Kingdom's very own Reg Park, whom the press dubbed 'Britain's Great Hope.'

There were six selected judges and among them were a Belgium, Russian, Egyptian, Frenchman and Englishman that represented the international field. The Judge was Gregor Arax a very well-known and respected French physique photographer. George Greenwood was also a noted photographer. Andre Bouldard was the official delegate for the French Federation of Physical Culture, and Oscar Heidenstam served as chairman for the newly created National Amateur Bodybuilding Association, commonly referred to as NABBA.

Before the evening's event, all the competitors in the various classes met at the Scala Theatre for the preliminary judging. In the class one competition, four men quickly were identified as top contenders. George Dardene of Belgium, Hubert

Thomas the reigning Mr. Wales, Reg Park and Steve Reeves. While George Greenwood and other photographers snapped pictures, the judges studied the men as they posed one pose after the next. Finally, the judges handed in their final scores, the results of which would remain unknown until later on at the evening show.

After a lengthy break during which the contestants rested, ate dinner and prepared for their final night pose downs, everyone reassembled at the main theatre.

The 1950 Mr. Universe contestants. Reg Park and Reeves are seen at the top left of the stage of finalist. Courtesy Steve Reeves

Before an expectant crowd the winners were announced except for the class one division. The judge's final decision for first place in this class was an astounding replication of the 1948 Mr. Universe contest when Reeves and Grimek competed against each other ending in deadlock. This time it was Reeves and Reg Park. Each judge informed reporters that regardless of all the other class winners first and second place in the event rests between both Steve Reeves and Reg Park.

Chairman of the judges George Walsh covered the event for *Health & Strength* reporting, *"Two of the judges had found it impossible to separate the American and the Britisher and had recorded a joint vote for each. One vote had voted outright for Park and two had voted outright for Reeves."*

Once again, the two bodybuilders were called out on to stage and pose for the judges. As they made their way up to the platform the applause was deafening, a roar that grew to a crescendo when the two began their individual poses. This time there were no splits, flips, handstands or other unrelated acrobatics to hold back the flawless Reeves. His routine that day was said to be perfect, his poses unique and never to be duplicated. With a perfect V- shape physique Steve looked like a carefully crafted sculpture from the renaissance days.

The final two; Britain's Reg Park facing off to America's one and only Steve Reeves. Courtesy Steve Reeves

Years later, Arnold Schwarzenegger (three-time Mr. Universe, and six-time Mr. Olympia wrote in his book, *ARNOLD: The Encyclopedia Of A Bodybuilder,* "*Steve Reeves was one of the first bodybuilders to develop the classic 'V' shape. He was able to achieve this look because he had naturally wide shoulders and a small waist. Proportions like this help create the most aesthetic physiques in bodybuilding.*" Schwarzenegger noted that it was Reeves wide shoulder width which gave him an enormous advantage. "*It would have been foolish for me to attempt Steve Reeves's style of posing, the arms overhead kind of thing,*" Arnold added. "*Reeves had broad shoulders, a flat chest and narrow waist, and overhead poses suited him. Steve is one of the few bodybuilders to ever master the arms over the head pose. You need long legs, a very symmetrical body, a 'V' shaped torso with a small waist, wide shoulders, and an almost flat chest (which helps to show off your lats). It also helps to have a square, flat chested frame.)*"

Reeves and Park were called back for a second round of poses. When the sixth judge declared his decision, George Walsh stepped up to the microphone to announce the winner of the 1950 Mr. Universe. "*Ladies and gentleman, I give to you the 1950 Mr. Universe Mr. Steve Reeves of America!*" Reeves had won by a three to one margin.

As the crowd applauded, Reeves was presented with the bronze statuette of Sandow. (In 1977 Reeves acquired the other original gold edition of the Sandow trophy from French bodybuilder and actor Serge Nubret.

Nubret had learned that Reeves was interested in acquiring the gold statuette and originally purchased the statuette from another collector for five-thousand dollars. At the 1977 WABBA Championships in Paris, Serge Nubret gave Reeves the gold statuette edition for his contributions to the sport. The whereabouts of the third silver statuette version remains a mystery, *"Yeah, that silver one is probably sitting up in someone's attic right now as we speak."* Laughs Steve, *"And the people who own it, don't even know what they have."*

With the bronze statuette cradled in his arm and wearing his good luck ring (a ring Reeves had specially made from the melted gold from both Goldie's and Lester's wedding bands and remade into a new symbolic ring representing his parents) Steve delivered his acceptance speech. He then made a surprise announcement. In a quiet and graceful manner, Steve declared that he was retiring from competitive bodybuilding.

"I want to thank you all for all of your support and applause over the years," Reeves told the crowd, *"But I feel it it time to retire and leave competitive bodybuilding. I now want to pursue new goals of mine in other areas of interest. Thank you again for all your support and kindness."*

Although Reeves was comfortable with his decision, many others thought he retired too early. In 1965, Joe Weider wrote in *Your Physique* magazine, *"The greatest bodybuilder of all time I think was Steve Reeves, but I think he stopped serious training and competing before he reached his full potential."* When he decided to leave the sport of bodybuilding, Reeves was only twenty-four.

Reeves walked away without any regrets. *"I stopped competitive bodybuilding when there was no other place to go,"* he recalls. *"There was no Mr. Olympia contest at that time, like there is today. I stopped competing in order to earn a living. I accomplished what I set out to do. Well nearly everything. I wanted to achieve a twenty-four-inch difference between my chest and waist measurements and fell short of the mark by just one inch. I also wanted a shoulder breath of twenty-four inches. Armand Tanny measured me at twenty-three and a half, six more months of intensive training and I would have got that extra half-inch. Other than that, I have no regrets."*

From London, Steve flew back to America where two victory parties were thrown in his honor, the first in New York City at Sig Klein's gym, and then back in Santa Monica at Vic's Dungeon.

Eager to be back on the West Coast, Reeves purchased an old Ford convertible from a friend of John Grimek's and drove back West to California. He still harbored the dream of a movie career and with an instinctive understanding of timing, Reeves hoped to capitalize on the fame he had achieved. Although no longer a competitive bodybuilder and in the limelight, his name was golden to the tens of thousands around the world.

In Europe, the Reeves look was now the great look. Mandatory weight training was instituted at European ballet companies as well as the New York City Ballet. Weight lifting routines were incorporated into the training sessions as close as possible to that of Steve Reeves'. The ballet masters wanted their dancers to have a more masculine, stronger upper body to match their muscular lower bodies, making them more symmetrical, and synonymous with that of the Reeves look.

Although colleagues from the gym second guessed his decision to retire, Steve was ready to take on new challenges.

"There was more to life for me than just roaming the beaches, and lifting weights," Reeves says of this time in his life. *"I wanted more than that. I had already lived that life. I still wanted to act and star in movies. I wanted to see what was out there for me. I wanted to travel and see the world, and to experience as much as I could."*

The following month, Steve made the cover of *Health & Strength*, proving once again he was number one.

Even in his most imaginative vision, the young champion could not have foreseen all that lay ahead.

A 1952 publicity photo of Reeves. Courtesy Steve Reeves

CHAPTER ELEVEN

Experiments

"I knew Steve during a very frustrating period in his career. However, this filtered down to Steve's philosophy and his golden rule, 'you have to suffer to be great!' Steve must have said that a thousand times. He really believed in it."

- John Weidermann, Broadway actor

Although Reeves had already achieved more than most people accomplish in a lifetime, one goal remained unrealized, a career in the movies as a leading man. This dream would eventually be realized but not before he would travel a five-year path that would lead him through a stint in television, a pilot that never aired, his debut in a featured film, regional theatre, Broadway, summer stock, marriage and divorce.

After London and his stunning win over Reg Park, Steve returned home with a renewed enthusiasm to pursue his acting ambition. He again learned that producers were reluctant to risk money on a muscleman with dramatic aspirations. In the fifties there were no promoters or corporations with national clout to advance the field of physical culture. Joe and Ben Weider, two of the biggest promoters within the sport today were just beginning their careers.

Obviously, Reeves was not without name recognition. As holder of the titles of Mr. America, Mr. World, and Mr. Universe Reeves was extremely popular within the sport. When Bert Goodrich, a supporter of Reeves since they had first met at the 1947 Mr. Pacific Coast competition heard that he had permanently retired from competition and was looking for employment, so Goodrich immediately hired Steve as an assistant manager at his Hollywood gym, a smart move since having the current Mr. Universe on staff would prove to be a big draw business wise.

On July 1, 1950 Reeves began working at Goodrich's gym, an elaborate fitness facility located at 6624 Hollywood Blvd. The date was significant not only because it marked a new cycle in Reeves career but also because it would have been his father Lester's fifty-first birthday. Lester was still an inspiration to Steve and would often fuel Reeves' will, a silent motivation few of his colleagues in the gym or in life ever knew about.

During the year Reeves while working for Goodrich the rumors flew. As far north as Oakland, word spread that Steve was being paid up to one hundred dollars a day to manage the facility. Contrary to these rumors, Reeves was living in a modest apartment building one block down from the gym. It soon became evident to him that he needed a job that would guarantee more money and benefits. In the spring of 1951, Reeves was hired on at Lockheed as an assembler at the Beverly Hills plant, a job that would lose its appeal within weeks.

"When I signed on with Lockheed, they hired me as a rivet operator, riveting little plates and tiny parts all day. I told my foreman, who incidentally was a woman, don't you have any boxes or crates to be moved, something where I could lift and move things for ten minutes and rest for five? Sitting there all day, riveting was just too damn tedious for my taste. Man, I couldn't stand that kind of work. I was much more into manual labor and heavy lifting."

Additionally, Reeves had a conflict with the foreman. When Steve first signed on with the company, she had indicated that she liked him as more than just a fellow employee, but Reeves discouraged her, resulting in an uneasy dynamic around the plant. Reeves recalls, *"My manager knew I was not interested in dating her, so after those first couple of weeks, matters got worse. It was very uncomfortable knowing your boss is resenting you for not liking her, other than a work-based relationship."*

Reeves lasted with Lockheed for three months, staying on until September because the company promised workers that if they remained on the job for at least three months they would be guaranteed a job if they ever returned for employment.

Three days a week, Steve continued to train at Goodrich's occasionally working there on weekends as well. Then, one Monday morning in July a second show business break came for Steve, when who other than television host and star Ralph Edwards walked through the front door.

Edwards was a well-known radio producer and entertainer who had just finished his radio shows *This Is Your Life*, and *Truth Or Consequences* a program that ran for ten years. He was now developing a new project *The Ralph Edwards Show*, which was under contract with the fledgling NBC.

With casting for his new TV show almost complete, Ralph Edwards still had not found the right actor for the role of Steve Trell, a male fitness trainer, ironically. Edwards wanted someone who would not only look the part but could act as well. Ralph had heard from various sources that he should check out Goodrich's gym in Hollywood for possible leads. That Monday morning, unannounced Edwards walked into the gym to begin interviewing candidates.

Gordon Hanson, Bob Schwartz, and Eiferman, along with many of the other guys from Goodrich's and Vic's auditioned for the role, but from his initial meeting, Edwards was very impressed by Reeves' look and charisma. The bodybuilder's previous acting training gave him the added edge he needed over the others and won the role easily. From the very beginning, a shared history created a bond between the two. Like Reeves, Edwards had grown up in Oakland during the depression years and had also graduated from Castlemont High. Each had struggled trying to break into show business.

1951 was television's first year of general programming, and most of the shows originated in New York. *The Ralph Edwards Show* however was filmed in Los Angeles. It debuted September 1st. and aired on weekdays from 12:30 to 1:00 PM.

It was a great time for newcomers to break into the business. Television offered more roles for actors and commissioned more scripts from writers, roughly five-hundred dramas in 1952 alone, producing more than six years of Broadway productions. Because costs were minimal, the stakes were lower for producers. A host of talented people got their first breaks then, stars like Ozzie and Harriet Nelson, Lucille Ball, Dinah Shore, and Red Skeleton were all drawn to this new medium and its opportunities.

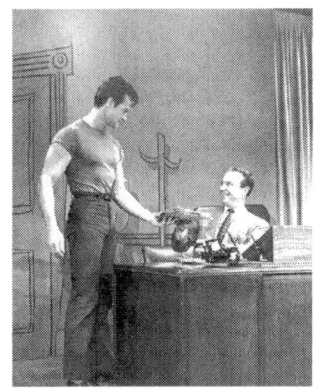 

Scenes from the 1951 *Ralph Edwards Show*. Courtesy Steve Reeves

Reeves's new agent was Helen Ainsworth. He signed on with her at the suggestion of a new friend, Guy Madison who was currently starring in the popular Western *Wild Bill Hickok*. Madison told Reeves that Ainsworth had landed him many roles in both television and film and encouraged Reeves to contact her with his portfolio.

In spite of the excitement surrounding the Edwards show Steve continued to work at Lockheed determined to stay past his three-month date. During the day, Reeves was on the set of NBC and at nights he worked his four to midnight shift at Lockheed, a schedule that was hectic and exhausting, but never once did he consider giving up. Staying at the plant was his insurance.

"I didn't want to burn my bridges with Lockheed, because as I have learned before in show business, anything can happen." Reeves says. "One day, you are big time, making all this money and working with other famous actors and actresses and then all of a sudden, in the blink of an eye, you are washed up and it's all over! Back then, most people my age had either a college *education, or a trade they had learned that they could fall back on. Where I, on the other hand, had nothing. Sure, I graduated from high school and served in the Army, won every professional bodybuilding competition there was, but that is all I had. Acting and making it in show business was my only hope at that time."*

From the beginning, *The Ralph Edwards Show* and Reeves was a big hit. A comedy series that centered around four characters. Edwards played a wealthy attorney, Carole Richards was his wife, Reeves was Steve Trell, a physical fitness trainer, and Jerry Lawrence rounded out the cast.

The show was shot live in Burbank. Edwards had a reputation in the industry for being zany and cast members were not exempt from his humor. Today, Reeves remembers being a victim of Edwards's humor. On April Fool's day before filming that day, Edwards appeared before the studio audience and told them not to laugh whenever Reeves told a scripted joke.

"When I arrived, Carol Richards told me that Ralph was unable to make it due to a sudden illness, and that I would have to take his part, so I did," smiles Reeves. *"I thought to myself 'no problem.' As the cameras started rolling, I told the band to play their first number, but they did not and the audience just sat there looking at me like I was a fool. I first thought, 'didn't they hear me?' so again I said play, and that time they began to play. Then it was time for me to begin telling jokes, but no one laughed so I thought, 'Okay, I'll get them with the next joke.' But no, no one laughed the second time, or the third time, finally I just looked over to the side where the camera guys were and said, 'What's up?' Well, halfway through the show, with me half soaking from nervous sweat, Ralph came running out onto the stage laughing and waving to the crowd, yelling, 'April fool's day Steve! April fool's!!' Well, everyone in the audience just broke down laughing*

along with probably everyone else in all of America watching that day. Yeah, Ralph really got me really good that time."

While at NBC, Steve worked with drama coach Natasha Lites. The classes comprised of six actors that were held weekly at Lite's home studio in Beverly Hills. Previously, she had been with 20th. Century Fox coaching among others than newcomer Marilyn Monroe.

The Ralph Edwards Show, although successful ran for only one year after which Edwards and his producers switched focus. They decided to take his previous radio show *This Is Your Life* and air it as a television program, a show that eventually ran from late 1952 to 1961, and then again from 1971 to 1973.

Although the Edwards show lasted only a year, it was an important break for Reeves. Fan response was enthusiastic. *"You should have read some of the letters that I had been getting back then,"* Reeves says. *"They were the craziest of notes. I even had women wanting to marry me!"*

In an amazing coincidence, on the adjacent set another was another actor with the last name of Reeves, a George Reeves who was starring in the newly syndicated series *The Adventures of Superman.* In the years ahead, their surnames would lead to many misunderstandings by fans who often confused the two actors or mistook them for brothers. Interestingly enough, George Reeves was his stage name, his real name was George Brewer.

Although *The Adventures of Superman* was a major hit, from the beginning tension escalated between the producers and their star. Occasionally, when they felt their Superman was getting out of control the producers threatened to release George and sign on the other Reeves, conveniently a few blocks away there in Burbank. They had repeatedly told George that Steve would be more than happy to sign on and play the part of Superman, and that

Steve would not need a padded suit for the role either. Consequently, George remained with the show but developed an intense grudge against Steve.

Although the two Reeves would each eventually play mythical characters, Superman and Hercules the individuals themselves could not have been more opposite. George Reeves' career only lasted from 1951 to 1959 when his final role of Superman in *The Adventures of Superman* stopped airing. Sadly, George suffered from depression due to his inability to land the sort of parts he wanted, which in turn led to his suicide that summer of 1959. Speculation, was that he took his life due to the immediate ending of his contract with ABC.

One month after his debut with *The Ralph Edwards Show*, Steve signed on with CBS to shoot a pilot for a half-hour mini series titled *Kimbar Lord of The Jungle*. The theme of the show was similar to that of another current series called *Tarzan*, starring Johnny Wiesmueller. However, after the pilot had been made, CBS turned it down. Due to production costs, the network was looking for a one-hour series. The half-hour pilot never aired.

In spite of this setback, Reeves's television career was taking off. From 1951 to 1954 in addition to *The Ralph Edwards Show*, Steve made cameo appearances on a number of popular programs including *The George Burns and Gracie Allen Show, Topper, The Red Skeleton Show, The Ozzie Nelson Show* and in 1953 *The Dinah Shore Show*.

As the first professional bodybuilder turned actor in Hollywood history, Reeves was proving to be a valuable statesman for the sport of bodybuilding. He was proving that the phrase, all brawn and no brain, a derogatory term often given to bodybuilders did not pertain at all. Countless times during television appearances, and in magazine articles Reeves pointed out that bodybuilders had gotten a bad rap. He was an articulate and passionate spokesman for the sport. Knowing the public perception of bodybuilders were that of men who talked only about lifting weights, ate pounds of meat, and twenty eggs a day, and even slept twelve hours replied in saying, *"That's not what bodybuilding is all about. Who wants to be part of that kind of sport?"* Reeves would stress the sense of accomplishment that he others received from weight training and exercising, adding that one should also have a life outside of the gym, and should have other interests as well.

By the mid 1950's Reeves's photographs had graced the cover of nearly a hundred magazines world-wide now, appearing more times than any other bodybuilder ever achieved. Steve's face on magazine covers not outperformed such greats as John Grimek, Reg Park and Clancy Ross now. Interest in Reeves spread to the general circulation magazines as well. In the March 1953 issue of *TAB* magazine, a periodical in the 1950's and 60's that was similar to today's *PEOPLE* magazine Reeves was described as 'the finely developed male Adonis in the country today,' and dubbed 'Mr. Sex Appeal.' He was also known as the 'king of bodybuilders.'

Additionally, Steve was a regular contributor to bodybuilding publications, work which proved to be his bread and butter at that time. Many of the cover shots were taken by Warner, Lanza and Paul Stone-Raymor leading photographers he had previously worked with. About this time, artist Hubert Stowitz was looking for a model for a new project, the twelve labors of Hercules. Reed Maxie, a bodybuilder who worked out at Goodrich's gym, knew the artist and arranged for Stowitz to meet Reeves.

Although the artist had no money to pay a model, Reeves agreed anyway. *"Something told me I must do this, so I did,"* he recalls. "Spiritually, I guess I knew I should do it. So, every

Thursday for two to three hours, for six month straight I drove over an hour up to Redondo Beach to pose for this twelve labours of Hercules art project. In 1957, when Steve landed the role of Hercules in Pietro Francisci's epic film, Reeves said he felt it was predestined and set in motion years before when he began posing for Stowitz. Years later, after the portraits were completed, Stowitz sold them to the oil billionaire J. Paul Getty for an undisclosed price. Getty was a tremendous admirer of Reeves and collected many other portraits of him, in addition to the Stowitz Hercules series.

In the fall of 1952, another career opportunity emerged. Steve was now dating a model by the name Barbara Sarrow, and had been in the show business for some time now knowing the market well. Barbara encouraged Steve to start trying out for some modeling jobs, even offering to contact her agent on his behalf. With his current bodybuilding portfolio in hand, Steve seemingly overnight landed jobs within the modeling industry, often modeling for articles on behalf of health and wellness. Another modeling job Steve landed was with Weber Bread company. Within weeks, Reeves' picture appeared in Weber bread ads in magazines and promotional posters. Reeves' photo turned up on everything from the sides of delivery trucks, to billboards along the major Calfornia highways.

1953 marked Steve's film debut. Director Edward D. Wood best known for his space epic *Plan Nine From Outer Space* was in the process of casting *The Hidden Face*, a crime thriller based on producer's Edward Small's 1935 film *Let'em Have It* (British title, *False Faces*) about a gangster who has his face altered by a plastic surgeon to elude the law.

Reeves' talent agent Ainsworth got him the role so that he could get his Screen Actors Guild card (SAG). Although it was a low budget production, Ainsworth believed it was an opportunity for Reeves to break into movie making.

Wood immediately took to Reeves and cast him for the part of Lt. Bob Lawrence in the film, eventually renamed *Jail Bait* as the producers felt *The Hidden Face* was not catchy enough for the market. Edward D. Wood screenwriter, pornographer, and hell raiser, was one of the most iconoclastic and tragic figures in Hollywood history proved to be a perfect director for the fledgling Reeves. In Rudolph Grey's book *Nightmare Of Ecstasy* a book based on the films of Edward D. Wood, Reeves was interviewed about his experience working with him. *"It was a pleasure to work with a director like Ed Wood. He was patient and understood how to make new and inexperienced actors feel at ease and get the best performance out of them."* Years later, Reeves added in another interview, *"Wood was especially flexible when it came to decision making, and worked extremely well with us, letting us try new methods of our own. Overall, I would have to say that Ed Wood was a very experimental director, and I liked that in him."* They began filming *Jail Bait* in February of 1953 and completed the cult film just three weeks later.

Images from Edward D. Wood's 1954 film *Jail Bait*, co-starring Steve Reeves. Courtesy Joe Sciambra

In late summer, a fellow actor handed Steve a script for *Kismet*. The musical drama based on Edward Knoblock's play and book by Charles Lederer and Luther Davis was straight out of the Arabian Knights. The Los Angeles Civic Light Opera Association was launching a remake of the 1911 original that starred Otis Skinner. On the advice of his agent, Reeves signed on in early October. For his supporting but showy role as one of the two Wazir guards, Steve was contracted for a salary of one-hundred and fifty dollars a week, including traveling expenses while on tour.

Following a month of rehearsals in Los Angeles, *Kismet* premiered in San Francisco then went on tour with performances in Denver, Cincinnati, Chicago, Detroit, Washington D.C., and Boston.

On December 3rd., 1953 *Kismet* opened at the Ziegfeld Theatre on Broadway. Although Steve's performance as a Wazir guard was small he did receive recognition from the critics for his duet 'Was I Wazir,' with fellow guard John Weidermann. *Kismet* didn't receive the kind of positive reviews producer Edwin Lester hoped for, although the shows choreography and set design did garner praise.

Steve stayed on with the show for over a year and a half and toured the East coast. While on the road, Reeves roomed with John Weidermann who was also a fitness enthusiast. In Milton T. Moore's photo leaflet titled *Steve Reeves, A Tribute,* Weidermann speaks of Reeves in those days, a time that was a blend of lighthearted freedom, and frustration *"We would be walking along in the city and suddenly Steve would halt me and say, 'take a picture of me here, John.' Steve would be standing beneath a sigh which would have a silly connotation or ironic application to it. I never saw Steve without humor,"* recalled Weidermann adding that humor was as much a part of Reeves's make-up as his honesty and sincerity. The actor also witnessed how Reeves coped with the inherent pressure of an acting career. *"I knew Steve during a very frustrating period in his career however this filtered down to his Golden Rule 'you have to suffer to be great! Steve must have said that a thousand times, he really believed in it. Steve understood what was going on around him, and he was on top of everything. I would not have thought of some of the things Steve zeroed in on. He had a special awareness of things that I certainly wasn't aware of at his age. It would have taken a person with tremendous power to influence Steve against his will. In working-out, or attaining any goal he set his mind to, Steve was extremely focused. When I knew him, he could not be steered in any direction he did not want to go."*

One of the dancers in *Kismet* was Neile Adams who at that time was dating Steve McQueen, another unknown trying to break into acting through the Broadway circuit as well. Often after the show, the cast would meet at Carnegie's Delicatessen and it was here that Reeves first met Steve McQueen. Adams introduced the two because she knew they both liked Westerns and wanted to someday star in one. Reeves recalls, *"My first impression of Steve McQueen was that he was kind of a bum. He dressed in ripped jeans and dirty t-shirts, just your plain simple street clothes. I guess he wasn't concerned or worried about impressing anyone. Actually, McQueen and I had a few things in common."* Their conversation centered on horses, cowboys and even fast drawing a pistol. *"I mean, this guy was unbelievable when it came to drawing a pistol,"* Reeves recalled. *"He would actually practice drawing a pistol in the streets, waiting in lines, or just standing around talking with us."* Just four years later McQueen earned the starring role of Randall, a fast drawing cowboy in the successful CBS television series *Wanted: Dead Or Alive*. We all know where McQueen's career went from there.

In early spring of 1954 during a break from *Kismet,* Reeves returned to the West Coast where he had landed a part in his second movie, a William Ludwig and Leonard Spigelgass film titled, *Athena* co-starring MGM stars Jane Powell, Edmund Purdom, Vic Damone, and Debbie Reynolds. When Director Joe Pasternak, known for his dazzling MGM musicals *The Great Caruso* and *Annie Get Your Gun,* met with Reeves he knew he had found the ideal actor for the role of chief muscleman. Instantly, Steve happily agreed to the project, and brought to the role everything he had to offer to the world of bodybuilding The role centered around a health oriented way of living, exercising and eating right. Today, more than six decades later the movie's message about the value of a healthy living is uncannily timely.

A publicity photo for MGM's 1954 film *Athena*. Pictured here is Edmund Purdom, Steve Reeves with Jane Powell and Debbie Reynolds atop his shoulders, and Vic Damone. Courtesy Steve Reeves

While in Los Angeles for the filming, Reeves lived on Hobart Street in the Hollywood area. Steve ended up renting a small guest house on the estate of Daniel Blum, a New York screen writer who met Reeves while he was on tour with *Kismet*, offering then Steve a place to stay back on the West Coast if he ever needed it.

In July, with filming *of Athena* completed Reeves appeared in his first summer stock production, Milton Lyon's, *Wish You*

Were Here. The show, staged in Sacramento was another opportunity to gain experience and be noticed by directors.

The play, performed outside was a light comedy about a group of young adults camping in the Catskills of upper state New York. The moral of the story centered around the notion of a lifetime of happiness that comes from summer romances. Reeves earned seventy-five dollars a week for his performance as none other than Muscles. The part was very showy, and much attention was paid to Reeves by critics following the play's opening at the Music Circus. Audiences responded to his charismatic stage presence, and the minute he made his entrance, they noisily flipped through their programs to learn his identity.

In the local paper, The Sacramento Bee, William Glackin reported, *"Steve Reeves, Mr. Universe, is of course a perfect piece of casting as Muscles, but he manages also to do a creditable job of creating character as well as looking it."*

Years later, Reeves said his performance in the comedy taught him an important lesson in acting. *"In the first scene, they had me walk out wearing a tank top, shorts and sneakers while bouncing a basketball. Well, the crowd went crazy clapping and cheering for me and I said my line, but apparently a cast member didn't hear me and said, 'say it again.' Well, the second night of the play's performance, I was so sure of myself from the opening applause the day before that I came out fully charged and expectant of the applause again but ended up not even getting twenty claps. That night, I learned that one should concentrate on one's role and the other actors, and not what is going on in the audience."*

Before he had to return to New York again for his touring with *Kismet*, Reeves had a few weeks left and decided to spend back in Santa Monica at the beach relaxing and working on his tan.

One day, while approaching a group of bodybuilders and their girlfriends, Reeves was drawn to a pretty brown eyed, brunette named Sandra Smith. Smith, born and raised in the San Fernando Valley and was eighteen years old, ten years younger than Reeves. Sandra was just beginning her senior year then in high school. Like his previous girlfriend Anita Sockle, Sandra was a part time model there in L.A.

Steve singled her out despite the age difference. Reeves saw something special in Sandra that the other women he dated never had - an understanding of who he really was. For the next three weeks the two were inseparable, and each night Steve sent Sandra special delivery cards.

Too soon it was time for Steve to return to New York. In late September, Sandra drove him to Los Angeles International Airport and the two said their goodbyes.

Back on Broadway, Reeves rejoined the show, saddened with the fact that he terribly missed Sandra.

A month later, Steve called Sandra and proposed. She accepted. After checking the performance schedule and waiting for Sandra to graduate from high school on January 28th, early that year due to her high enough earned credits the two settled on a wedding date of January 31 st, 1955.

The couple were married at the United Methodist Church in Sherman Oaks, California in the San Fernando Valley with a reception following at the home of Sandra's parents.

Because of his Broadway commitment, there was no honeymoon and on their wedding night the newlyweds flew back east.

On the left, Steve's step-father Earl with Sandra, Steve and mother Goldie on Reeves wedding day. On the right, Sandra and Steve celebrating their wedding day together. Courtesy Steve Reeves

In the spring of 1955, there was an opening for a show girl in *Kismet* and Steve arranged through the director for Sandra to audition for the part. *"All she had to do was try out."* Reeves recalls, *"I got Sandra this great part, but she didn't want anything to do with it. She felt the part was too flashy and she didn't feel comfortable in front of large crowds."* This difference in temperament was later to become an on-going issue in their marriage.

In late fall, *Kismet* closed. By mid-October Steve learned from friends about casting of a new production soon to open in November, starring Carol Channing.

The show, *The Vamp* opened on November 10th., 1955 at the Winter Garden with Reeves playing the role of Samson. The production was about a farm girl turned glamorous actress working in a burlesque during the early days of film. One month after *The Vamp* premiered in spite of a large budget and good production values, it closed, unfortunately.

Carol Channing recalls of this time, *"Working with Steve in The Vamp was very nice. He was especially supportive to me, especially when the production began to take a dive. The Vamp didn't have a chance other than its huge budget. Our costumes which were designed and made by Raoul Pene were extravagant and beautiful, but really the only thing that held the show together. Robert Alton who choreographed the show was great. Actually, I believe it was Alton who gave Steve the script and hired him for his part. Alton put the show together in Washington and went on tour ending in New York. Unfortunately, Alton died between Washington and New York, which at that point, I believe was when the show suffered. The Vamp didn't really have a great director (David Alexander) and therefore there was very little hope. But working with Steve Reeves in the production, well he was great! I remember that Steve was an extremely focused and intelligent actor. He was always there on time and was always trying to learn and absorb as much as he could with his acting. It was a pleasure working with him."*

In January, with no contracts or deals in hand with his acting career, Reeves decided to head south to warm weather. He and Sandra bought an old station wagon, packed up everything they owned and headed to Fort Lauderdale, Florida.

Almost immediately conflicts arose between he and Sandra. Reeves being experienced and confident, was focused on his next goal of opening a business of his own. Sandra, on the other hand was still young, insecure and missing her family. After much discussion, they decided she should drive back to California and stay with her family in Studio City for a few weeks.

Alone in Florida now, Steve began looking for the ideal business opportunity. A young law student approached him about buying his gym and after negotiating the price, Reeves purchased it in February. Within three months of opening, *The Steve Reeves Gym* located at 6th. and Alton street immediately boasted an impressive membership of several hundred.

Meanwhile, Sandra was having a difficult time in California. When she talked with Steve she expressed loneliness and Steve sympathetically encouraged her to return to Florida.

In spite of the success of the gym, Reeves was restless. He had always dreamed of traveling and seeing exotic countries. While working at his gym, he would read articles in National Geographic about places like Australia, India and especially South America and imagined exploring and traveling to these unique locations. He borrowed books from the library and sitting on the gym's front step passionately studied these foreign destinations for hours on end.

Steve would often discuss his passion for travel with Sandra, and several times talked about the two of them just packing up, selling the car, and heading off for the countries he had read about. Sandra, wanting to settle down in a more traditional lifestyle, could not picture herself traveling. Reeves recalls, *"I was still young when Sandra and I got married in 1955 and the last thing I wanted to do was to be shackled down. I had not yet seen parts of the world that I had always dreamed of, so when Sandra made it very clear that traveling to say New Zealand or Venezuela did not appeal to her, among other things we talked about, we both decided that a divorce would be the best thing."*

On September 4th at the court house in Dade County, Steve and Sandra made it final, they were now divorced. Although no longer married, the two remained friends. Years later Sandra Smith told movie collector Milton T. Moore, Jr., *"My marriage to Steve was a fantastic experience for a young girl. I was very much in love with Steve, and he was a wonderful husband. Steve loved children and wanted children of his own more than anything in the world. Everything he has today was planned, and hoped for, years in advance, and his success came through great effort and sacrifice and was greatly deserved."*

Reeves was now focusing on new horizons, rather than traveling to exotic lands. He was again developing the itch to give show business another shot. Within days his divorce to Sandra, he put his gym on the market and it immediately sold the facility to a gym member, a college student whose parents put up the money.

In mid-September, Reeves returned to California.

The goal that had inspired him for almost ten years through three world titles, summer stock, television, two cameo roles in movies, and two Broadway plays refused to die, and now once again pulled Reeves back westward.

Reeves arriving in Rome prior to filming *Hercules*, 1957. Courtesy Steve Reeves

CHAPTER TWELVE

Hercules

"It was a question of the right person with the right face for the right part at the right time."

- Steve Reeves, Newsweek 1959

Soon after he returned to California, Reeves landed a job with *American Health Studios*, the largest chain of health gyms in the country at this time. The owner, and founder was Ray Wilson, the same Ray that Steve and Bob Weidlich had played practical jokes on ten-years earlier at Ed Yarick's gym.

"At this point in my life I had real direction now, and I could see things working for me," Reeves recalls.

Wilson contacted Reeves and offered him a position as public relations man, a job that entailed attending openings and spreading the word about American Health Studios.

"They had me as their number one man at all of their grand openings. Wherever there were ribbons to be cut, I was the guy

next with the good-looking girl at the ceremony." Steve says. *"Ray made me promise him that I give up show business if I wanted to stay with his company."*

The arrangement was working well for both Reeves and Wilson, and they began to talk about retirement plans for Steve along with other benefits. By the spring of 1957, Reeves had somewhat given up his goal of becoming a movie career, but not entirely. What he could not have known was that at the moment in Italy, a director by the name of Pietro Francisci was making a decision that would dramatically change Steve's life forever.

Francisci was known in Europe for making low-budget, epic movies. For nearly five years, the Italian director who had long admired films about Greek mythology had combed the world trying to find the right actor to play the title role in his latest project *Le Fatiche Di Erode* English subtitle being *Hercules*. He had contacted a number of American actors in Europe, but they were all currently contracted with other films in production. Ironically, Francisci had even considered Victor Mature, the actor who ten years earlier had taken over the part of Samson in Cecil B. DeMille's epic *Samson And Delilah* following Paramount's release of Reeves. To date, Pietro had not yet found the actor who matched his idea of the mythical muscleman.

Then one day, Francisci's thirteen-year old daughter who had just returned from seeing MGM's *Athena* currently playing in full houses throughout Europe, told her father, *'Papa, I think I have found your Hercules.'* Francisci saw the movie himself and knew his extensive search had ended.

For Reeves, the letter sent from Italy was confusing. It seemed that a successful European film company called *Lux-Titanus* was about to make a mythological film in Rome and wanted to contract Steve for the title role. Producer Federico Teti had raised one-hundred and ten thousand U.S. dollars to produce the film and directed by a forty-five-year old Italian by the name of Pietro Francisci.

Although content with his job at American Health Studios, Reeves had decided to forget about being an actor. He was not impressed with Francisci's letter. *"By that time in my career, I was so used to receiving offers that never materialized that I didn't dare allow myself to become excited."* recalls Steve. *"So, I didn't respond, not knowing if this Francisci was serious or might be offering a one-shot deal with not much money in it."*

A few weeks later he received a follow-up letter from Italy, and then an urgent telegram. When Steve opened the envelope, he discovered a round trip air ticket, a five-thousand U.S. dollar advance for his salary, and a contract to star in *Hercules* which was to be filmed in Rome beginning that June. *"I thought to myself, these people are serious!"* remembers Reeves.

On reflection, he decided the offer was too good to be refused. It was an opportunity to see a part of Europe Reeves had never seen, and to receive a starring role in a film. This was what Reeves had been aiming for ever since his training days at Stella Adler's Acting school, to be a leading man in a movie. Although Steve did not speak a word of Italian, and was somewhat leery about promises made in Hollywood, he called Francisci and accepted, asking what he needed to do to prepare himself.

"Grow a beard." the Francisci told him.

Without informing anyone, Reeves began planning for his trip overseas. Although still working for Wilson, he began growing a small goatee and mustache. When Wilson questioned him about the facial hair, Reeves convinced him that the beard made him appear more dignified and boosted his effectiveness on the job. *"I wasn't about to let Ray know that I was once again ready to take off on another wild goose chase. Too many movie opportunities had already turned out to be canards for me"* said Reeves.

A month later Reeves boarded a TWA flight to Rome.

The cast and crew of *Hercules* gathered at *Titanus-Lux* studios in Rome, and principal photography began shooting in early summer of 1957. Director of photography was the famed cinematographer Mario Bava. Except for a translator, Reeves was the only person on the set who could speak fluent English.

The shooting schedule, which would take nearly three months had been divided into two parts. Exteriors would be shot on location just north of Rome in a small town called Anzio, overlooking the Mediterranean. With its cliffs and barren landscape, it was an ideal setting to replicate ancient Greece. There, under very primitive conditions the crew found themselves enacting spectacular scenes, including Reeves as Hercules uprooting a tree to stop a runaway chariot.

For the first part of filming interiors were shot in a large studio hangar at *Titanus*. These scenes included Hercules defying the gods while asking for his mortality and the climactic scene of him tearing down the mammoth pillars outside the temple. A still photo of this scene is the classic Hercules, the quintessential Reeves.

During this key fight sequence, Reeves swung chains hanging from his wrists to ward off the soldiers attempting to capture him. Steve remembers Fracisci yelling at him in broken English saying, *'Hit them harder. Why aren't you hitting them harder with those chains?'* Hesitantly, Reeves confronted the director.

"Even though the chains were carved out of wood, I tried to explain to him, with the aid of our translator that they still would

hurt them." Reeves recalls. *"But Pietro just yelled back at me, 'you hit them, you hear me, they are paid to be hit! So, I did, but still not as hard as Francisci wanted me to."*

Reeves with co-star Sylva Koscina in *Hercules*, 1957. Steve in his signature Hercules pose during the film ending. A full sheet movie poster from the mega block buster. Courtesy Steve Reeves and Joe Sciambra

In Milton T. Moore's photo booklet *Steve Reeves, A Tribute,* Francisci said, *"Steve was very serious in his work, showed tremendous discipline and most of all engaged himself in a hard way. He moved into the character he played and lived there. Steve had an alarmingly handsome face that blended perfectly with history's most perfect physique. Through the expression of his face he could communicate to audiences that his mind was deep in thought and far away from the events that were occurring around him. He seemed at times to be contemplating things beyond the comprehension of other ordinary individuals around him."*

By the time *Hercules* was complete, the cast and crew were exhausted from the nearly three-month shoot. In fact, everyone involved in the production had taken their share of bumps and bruises, including Reeves who had done all of his own stunts. With the principal photography complete, Francisci returned to the *Lux-Titanus* in Rome to begin the post production and editing process. The final score by Enzo Masetti was recorded. The schedule release date for Hercules throughout Europe was slated for late August 1957.

At this point Reeves, who was somewhat skeptical about the film, had no idea of what was to become of the production. Still feeling some of the injuries he received while performing his own stunts, Steve needed a vacation and made plans for a trip to Majorca, Spain. He shaved his beard and stayed in Rome for one more week since his contract did not run out until another week. The day of his departure, Reeves received a phone call from Francisci who was not pleased with several of the film's scenes and wanted to re-shoot them. But there was a catch. The film had already gone over its projected budget, thus there was no money left to pay the cast for another day of filming.

Reeves recalls, "Pietro's only words to me over the phone were, *"Steve, if you were my friend you would do it for nothing!"* and I replied, *"Well if you were my friend, you would not ask me to do it for nothing."* Later Steve added, *"Pietro Francisci was probably the best director I ever worked with. He had some really great ideas and notions about making a movie, but at the end of filming Hercules he simply was flat broke!"*

Reeves agreed to stay on for an additional week so that Francisci could fully complete the filming of the epic adventure. Although he may have may have been disappointed about having to stay on in Rome, the rescheduling was to change his life in another area.

At the Madison House, a popular restaurant in Rome a cocktail party was being held to celebrate the completion of filming. There, Reeves met the woman who would become his next wife.

Aline Czartjarwitz was a twenty-four-year old, blue-eyed, blond that had heard of the party from a mutual friend. Aline had been educated in Switzerland and worked in the European film industry as a legal aid dealing with contracts. She was a princess, the daughter of an aristocratic Polish family. Her father, an avid anti-communist had been killed as a result of his political activities.

Aline had not planned on going to the party, but her cousin persuaded her to attend. *"The place was packed,"* Aline recalled during an interview in a 1983 issue for *Muscle & Fitness* magazine. *"Somehow, I got separated from my cousin and when I wanted to leave I could not find him."* When she started off in search of her relative, Aline heard an appealing male voice and turned to see the most handsome man she had ever seen.

She watched a different man from the Iranian embassy approach Reeves who had heard through others at the party of Reeves bodybuilding accomplishments and asked him, *'Is it true Sir that you eat a kilo of steak at every meal?'* When Steve answered no, the Iranian seemed surprised to learn that the muscular stranger ate normal portions. Then Aline did say something that later on she would consider quite silly. She asked Steve, *'If one wanted to invite you for half a kilo of steak, where would one find you?'* Reeves smiled and informed Aline that he was staying at the American Palace.

Later that night Aline asked her cousin if he had noticed the stranger's eyes.

'Eyes,' he said. *'Did you see his shoulders?'*

'Obviously padded,' Aline retorted. On learning of the stranger was the Steve Reeves she said, *'Then for certain I will invite him to dinner.'*

'Are you crazy?' responded Aline's cousin, *'That man is the toast of Rome. He won't have time for you.'* But he did.

Years later in an interview Reeves recalled his first impressions of Czartjarwitz. *"Aline was extremely charming, and very pretty,"* he recalls. *"She had it all. I was especially impressed that she could speak six languages fluently."*

They dated that week, and then Steve not believing he would ever see her again boarded a flight for his delayed vacation to Majorca. At this point, Reeves thought once again his movie career was over. On completion of *Hercules*, he had not been offered an extensive contract nor was any sequel planned. Following his stay in Spain, Steve returned to Los Angeles.

Back in California, Reeves convinced Wilson to rehire him, promising to work twice as hard. After much skepticism on Ray's behalf, Steve signed on once again with American Health Studios, but this time at half the salary working this time as a salesman in San Diego where a new gym was being built.

Steve had not spent much time in Southern California and found the climate and terrain very appealing. Soon he was looking for real estate and found one location that interested him. A fourteen-acre lot that was sited just outside Escondido in a small town called Valley Center, just fifty miles Northeast of San Diego was priced at fifteen thousand dollars. The location was convenient to the mountains, airports, and ocean, and in a perfect climate for growing avocados, a favorite fruit of Steve's. Additionally, the area was a great place for raising horses. After much consideration, Reeves put down five-thousand dollars of his ten-thousand-dollar earnings from *Hercules*. *"It was one of the best decisions I ever made,"* Reeves told *The Los Angeles Times*.

While he continued to work for American Health Studios, word began to get back to him from Europe that *Hercules* was really taking off successfully at the box offices. In Italy, Hercules had out grossed both James Dean's latest film *Giant,* and *The Bridge Over The River Kwai*. Within a week of its release in Italy and France, the film had earned back its expenses. Eventually, *Hercules* would go on to earn more than fourteen-million dollars, over half of these earnings were in Europe. In spite of its success overseas, no American release date of the film had been scheduled. Reeves continued working in San Diego, unaware of what lay next for his European debut. Years later, friends Steve made back in Europe told Steve that they would have informed him about the film's success if he only he had stayed in touch with them.

This would prove costly. In March of 1958, Reeves agent Mitchell Gertz knowing how well *Hercules* was doing signed Steve on for a sequel titled *Hercules Unchained* that was to begin filming that summer. One of the terms, unknown to Reeves was a contract bonus for only Gertz of a first class, round trip ticket around the world with full accommodations.

After an unpleasant parting from Wilson, Reeves flew to Rome to begin filming *Hercules Unchained*. Again, the screenplay was written by Francisci. *"Steve was very serious in his work, showed tremendous discipline, and most of all engaged himself in a hard way. He moved into the character he played and lived there."* Francisci said in Milton T. Moore, Jr.'s *Steve Reeves, A Tribute*.

Upon his arrival in Rome, Steve received a letter from his mother Goldie praising him for all his hard work and determination. *'God has been good to you,'* she wrote. *'Keep him that way.'*

"*My mom knew me pretty well,*" Reeves says. "*At times, when I would get way too confident with myself around other people, she knew just how to bring me down and discourage me from being that way. And when I was down, she knew just how to bring me back up, and motivate me.*"

In the meantime, Aline had not heard from Steve since he left for the U.S. in September of 57'. Soon after he arrived back in Rome in the spring, Steve and Aline resumed their friendship primarily, that in turn years later become a perfect union, both personally and professionally.

While the filming continued in mid-summer of 1958, others were beginning to pick up on the idea of filming other *Hercules* epics, often blatant copies of Francisci's big hit. Some the take offs were well made, but most were not.

"*Just after I arrived in Italy to begin filming Hercules Unchained, we began noticing other crews like ours, two and three beaches down from us, setting up cameras and filming Hercules films just like ours. It was unbelievable. They were using the same costumes, plots and even ideas as Francisci.*" Later Reeves added. "*I guess it was like anything else in life, once someone gets a great idea everyone wants in on it.*"

News of Steve's return to Rome was noted by the European newspapers. Everywhere Steve went he was followed by adoring fans, and paparazzi who recorded his every move for the world press.

In spite of the adulation, Steve found filming lonely at times. "*It was quite difficult,*" he recalls. "*I was working with people who barely spoke English."* At this time, Reeves was single and believed he would never date Aline again.

The sensual chemistry between Reeves and twenty-six-year old costar Sylvia Lopez in *Hercules Unchained* was very intense during filming, as well as off screen. Courtesy Steve Reeves

Starring opposite Steve was glamorous French actress and model Sylvia Lopez portraying the wicked Queen of Lydia in *Hercules Unchained*. What many people never knew about Steve and Sylvia is that their scripted romance carried on well off screen. *"Sylvia and I were very romantic off set as well."* Reeves said of his relationship with Lopez. *"She was a very sexual woman. We spent a lot of romantic time together, going out to dinner, sight-*

seeing and such. And then there was the sex… I'll say this much, Sylvia stayed the night over at my place a lot…I had no complaints, that's for sure." Unfortunately, just months after the completion of Hercules Unchained, the twenty-six-year old Lopez passed away due to Leukemia. Reeves added, *"…If Sylvia had not died the two of us may have remained together, who knows?"*

Meanwhile, *Hercules* was beginning its long road to the American silver screen do to the imagination of a highly successful producer, Joseph E. Levine.

Born in 1906 in Boston, Massachusetts the son of a poor tailor, Joseph Levine drifted from job to job. Salesman, shopkeeper, restaurateur, driving instructor, art theatre owner, Levine tried them all. He had invested in many companies, one of which was a drive-in theatre in Springfield, where he fell in love with movies. Soon he drifted into movie distributing and his talent for what he calls 'the big, big sell' began to pay off. Levine discovered where the money was now to be made, and it was in showing international movies here in the states. A film titled *Godzilla*, an Oriental chiller he discovered in Japan in 1955 was where it began for the local promoter. Levine was also drawn to a film titled *Attilla,* a hot action movie he picked up while in Italy two years later.

Until Levine entered the scene, *Hercules* was just another Italian film that several U.S. distributors had seen and sneered at, dismissing Reeves as just another refugee from California's Muscle Beach. On a tip, Levine flew to Rome in mid-1958 to view the film at *Lux-Galatea* studios with the interest of purchased the distribution rights. He was swept away upon its viewing. Later he enthusiastically told a *TIME* reporter, *"It had action and sex, a near shipwreck, gorgeous women on an island and a guy tearing a damn building apart. And where did you ever see a guy with a body like Reeves has?"*

In January of 1959 Levine purchased *Hercules* for a paltry one hundred and twenty thousand U.S dollars. He then brought it back to the States and dubbed it in English.

Levine budgeted 1.2 million dollars of his own money to spend for publicity. He had a zany imagination and devised every kind of campaign imaginable; Hercules comic books, Herculean Hamburgers, Test-Your-Strength machines strategically spotted in key-cities with Levine ensuring a charitable contribution every time some local muscleman rang the bell. Before Levine was finished $300,000 of the $1.2 million was spent on TV and radio ads alone. The fortitude and ingenuity Levine manifested in his *Hercules* campaigns were unrivaled for that time. He spent $350,000 on newspaper ads and $40,000 on an extravagant luncheon on the grand ballroom of Manhattan's Waldorf Astoria Hotel which was decorated with two-story silken banners bearing the image of Steve Reeves.

Not fully content with his promotions, Levine decided to mail out seven-hundred statues of Reeves to the nation's top critics. The figures, comprised of four pounds of chocolate were considered arrogant and offensive by several of the movie reviewers, and one of them wrote that they left it outside to melt in the sun until he thought it resembled Levine.

In May 1959 *Hercules* premiered at the Paramount theatre in downtown Hollywood, California and by mid-August the film was the largest box-office smash in Hollywood's memory to date. In its first week, *Hercules* opened in 145 neighborhood movie houses drawing in nine-hundred thousand dollars. In its second week, a total of six-hundred Eastman reels were now ready to be distributed, the largest order *Pathe Labs* had ever produced, and

Joseph E. LeVine's dazzling *Hercules* banquet held in March of 1959, at New York City Waldorf Astoria Hotel, boasted two story marquee banners highlighting Reeves as Hercules.

soon the film was simultaneously playing at one-hundred and twenty-five theatres in the New York area alone. All of Levine's efforts had truly paid off, turning what might have been a somewhat successful film, into a legend. Eventually Levine's one-million, two-hundred thousand-dollar investment had taken in more that fourteen-million dollars.

It was the granddaddy of what was to be called the Sword-and-Sandal genre films.

At this time, Steve's previous lady friend he met Aline was still working for Embassy Pictures who was Levine's new film promotion company. Her primary job now was to assist in promoting *Hercules,* including driving Cadillac's in parades with *Hercules* banners draped over the doors and hoods. When the film debuted, Aline arranged for Goldie and Steve's step dad Earl to join her at the opening in San Diego. This would be the first time Goldie would see her son Steve up on the silver screen. In one particular scene early on in the movie Hercules raises his arms in defiance to the gods. The sight of Steve standing in his classic pose caused Aline to yell out saying, *'Oh, my word!'* Until that point, she had never seen him without a shirt on. *"I had no idea his muscles were that big. I had always assumed they were just pads in his jacket,"* Aline recalled in an interview with *Muscle & Fitness* magazine.

The film's reviews were as glowing as the box office numbers;

"The best thing about Hercules seems to be those rippling muscles of Steve Reeves. I don't think I have ever seen such powerful fluidity in any picture, dating from silent films until now. Victor Mature's physique in the role of Samson seems puny compared to that of the gorgeously stacked Steve... He looks like the kind of man-half-god who just might have gone through some of the adventures set down in this story."

- Marjory Adams, *Boston Globe Herald*

"Hercules in the figure of Steve Reeves, and I do mean figure is taller, bigger, heavier, and at the same time smaller around the waist than any hero you have ever seen. Or any human being."

- Ruth Waterbury, *Los Angeles Herald Examiner*

*"That legend and spectacle go together like Castor and Pollox is demonstrated on a grand scale in Hercules, which was packing them into the Pilgrim Theatre yesterday. The public loves the super-man legend, and Hercules starring Steve Reeves, with

his mythological feats, which contain just enough of the human quality is certainly one of the most popular."

- Alta Maloney, *Boston Globe*

That summer, Steve Reeves became 1959's number one box-office star in America, as well as in twenty-six European countries, the Middle East and Australia edging out Rock Hudson, Doris Day and John Wayne Hollywood megastars who over the years had shared the title.

In spite of the film's raging success, Reeves thought little of the low-budget epic and was casual about his own role in its triumph. *"It was a question of the right person, with the right face, for the right part, at the right time,"* Reeves told *Newsweek* in 1959. *"Of course, my muscles helped, but my face was important, too. It had to be a typical American-boy face, a sympathetic one, like me. If a man has a tough face and gets into a tough spot, people say it served him right; tough face, tough spot, tough guy, see what I mean? But it you have a sympathetic face, they are sympathetic."*

Although it was fashionable to scoff at the cheap look of the film at the time, as well as its amateur dubbing *Hercules* out grossed all of the other twenty-three Hercules films that soon followed, creations of other Italian and American producers who desperately tried to match Francisci's achievement. Bodybuilders such as Mickey Hargitay, Reg Park, Lou Ferrigno and Arnold Schwarzenegger took their turn at the role, but no one could match the both the look nor the success of the Reeves original.

Eventually *Hercules* would go on to play all over the world, reportedly even behind the Iron Curtain and its run continued until well into the mid 1960's.

The success of the film caught its creators largely by surprise and made a cult figure of its young star. After more than ten years of striving, ten years of sacrificing, ten years of opportunities that turned into disappointments, Reeves was at last a leading man. For the next thirteen-years Steve went on to star in fourteen additional films, making his mark in both Hollywood and European film history as the first bodybuilder turned actor, while inspiring numerous bodybuilders who held the dream of an acting career - men like Arnold Schwarzenegger, Dolf Lundgren, Jean-Claude Van Damme, and Sylvester Stallone.

In a 1978 *Playboy* magazine interview Stallone said, *"I got interested in bodybuilding from one movie. I remember seeing things like On The Waterfront, and I had always end up in a deep snore. But one day I saw Steve Reeves in Hercules Unchained and I thought, Hey, it's one thing for Brando to stand up to the union, but this weird guy with the beard and big calves can pull down a temple all by himself. He is able to take on an entire Roman army using only the jawbone of an idiot then I'd like to do that, too."*

And in a 1991 *Parade* magazine Sylvester Stallone was quoted, *"The day I saw Steve Reeves was the day my life changed. It was like seeing the Messiah. I said, this is what I want to be.'"*

Reeves was now at the top of his game.

A celebration party for the completion of 1960 *Giant of Marathon*, seen here is co-star Daniella Roca with Steve and co-star Mylene Demongeot.

CHAPTER THIRTEEN

Unchained & Running

"Steve Reeves has developed into the most popular figure of heroic action on the worlds screen since Errol Flynn."

- William Wereth, *Motion Picture Herald* 1960

During the next ten years, Reeves made thirteen films. It was a time in film referred to as the Sword & Sandal classics. These movies, although hastily shot in Europe with poor scripts, were important in the development of cinema, especially Italian film making. Directors such as Sergio Leone and cinematographers Mario Bava owe much of their early development to their experience working on these films.

With his third starring movie *The White Warrior,* Reeves earnings had more than doubled now to twenty-five thousand dollars. By today's standards, his salary per film was minuscule, and Steve knew the film companies were financially reaping his own earnings. The mere mention of his name though, would clearly bring immediate attention and interest from producers making his films extremely marketable worldwide. People thronged to theatre's whenever it was announced that he was going to make a personal appearance.

In 1960, journalist John Ginfreddi wrote in the Italian magazine *Scene* about a typical Reeves public appearance. *"One by one, big limousines pulled up in front of Milan's plush Rudolph Theatre for the world premiere of the widely ballyhooed Hercules Unchained. Lining both sides of the theatre, a crowd of women was held in check by two rows of Milan police. When a big black Mercedes pulled up and a brawny, broad shouldered, bearded man stepped out, a full-throated roar rose from the crowd. Milan's police braced themselves against the wave of screaming, hysterical women. Then the surging women broke their ranks and swarmed over the hero in an orgy of adulation before the police could reform into a flying wedge that bulldozed through the crowd..."*

From now on, Reeves would star in two pictures a year. His shooting schedule usually began in the beginning of March for his first film and finish up in early June. Upon completion Steve would travel to Spain or Portugal for the following months and practice his equestrian skills. By August filming would again commence for his second film and completing in early November.

With the increasing popularity and earnings from *Hercules* and *Hercules Unchained,* producers such as Levine naturally wanted to make a third sequel. Levine first met with Reeves on the set of *The While Warrior* in the fall of 1959, this being Reeves' fifth movie to date including *Jail Bait* and *Athena.* Levine ended up convincing Steve while there to sign on to a two-movie contract deal. Naturally, Levine was hoping for another *Hercules* sequel, but this never happened. The films Reeves eventually made with

Levine were *Morgan The Pirate* and *The Thief Of Baghdad,* both filmed during the next two years.

The first post *Hercules* film Steve starred in was with *Majestic* Films in 1959 titled *The White Warrior.* Reeves portrayed a rebel commander named Hadji Murad in *The White Warrior.* The script was adapted from the novel *Hadji Murad* written by world renowned Russian novelist Leo Tolstoy. The story is based on actual events from the true life revolutionary Murad himself, highlighting on various parts of his life as a proud Chechen resisting the Russian government during the mid-1800's. Drawn to by the strong story line, and the immense success of Reeves two previous *Hercules* films, Director Riccardo Freda more than willingly agreed to take on the picture.

Giorgia Moll with Reeves during a scene from *The White Warrior*, 1959. The American Technicolor movie poster for *The White Warrior.* Courtesy Steve Reeves

As he did in the majority of his films, Reeves performed all of his own stunts just as he had in *The White Warrior.* Steve's equestrian skills enhanced his character's roles, therefore reducing production costs since stunt doubles were rarely used. Freda and Steve worked well together throughout the production, recalls Reeves. *"Riccardo Freda was a very good director. He explained the scenes perfectly, like he was a friend instead of a director."* Riccardo was particularly successful at choreographing and capturing large, and suspenseful action scenes many times on their first take.

Reeves on horseback performing his own stunts in *The White Warrior*, 1959.
Courtesy Steve Reeves

Co-star actress Giorgia Moll, an Italian model and actress starred beside Reeves creating a magical combination on screen for adoring fans in *The White Warrior*. Two years later, Moll would again team up with Steve in Arthur Lubin's 1961 classic remake of *The Thief of Baghdad*. This would be Giorgia's ninth movie to date upon starring in *The White Warrior*. Eventually, her most critically acclaimed and dramatic performance would be in the 1960 Italian crime-drama film *Lipstick*.

The majority of filming for *The White Warrior* took place in Yugoslavia due in part to its mountainous terrain, therefore reducing production costs by eliminating set designs within the studios. As with most of Steve's films, *The White Warrior* boasted extravagant costumes and plush set designs. With a mere budget of only five-hundred thousand Freda proved able at constructing set designs and props needed for the recreations of the glamorous Russian Czar of that time.

For Reeves' next role as Emilio in *Goliath and The Barbarians* this part could not have been a near carbon copy of the ever so popular *Hercules* character, complete with full beard, animal garments and flexing physique. Set in the year 568 AD in Northern Italy, the story is about a humble, woodsmen, Emilio who suddenly finds himself fighting to avenge the horrific murder of his father who was slain by savage barbarians from the northern mountains.

Co-star Chelo Alonso, a Cuban born dancer, and sultry actress well known for her 1960s cult film heroine and sex symbol in the U.S played the part of Landa in *Goliath and The Barbarians*. Alonso began her career as an exotic dancer at the *Folies Bergere* in Paris and went on the star in nineteen international films. Her most widely distributed movie would be that of *The Good, The Bad & The Ugly,* starring Cling Eastwood in 1966. This be Alonso's first of two films working alongside Reeves, as the following year the two would pair up again in Andre De Toth's 1960 classic *Morgan The Pirate*.

A *Goliath & The Barbarians* lobby card. Steve lifting Chelo Alonso into the air during a celebration of its last day of filming. A marquee sign displays the opening of *Goliath* in Time Square New York City. Courtesy Steve Reeves

During one particular battle scene in *Goliath and The Barbarians* Reeves ended up being severely cut by a sword from one of the other cast members. The result, a deep laceration to his left hand and wrist requiring over twenty stitches. Just seconds after being slashed from the sharpened sword (oddly enough on the set, and not intended for stage use) Steve yelled out in broken Italian, *'Buona notte a tutti!'* meaning *'goodnight everyone!* and that he was done for the day.

Unfortunately, *Goliath and The Barbarians* did not turn the kind of numbers at the box-office it had hoped to internationally, but still managed to turn a profit in both Japan and Western Europe.

In his next film Reeves played Glaucus in *The Last Days of Pompeii* co-starring with Austrian-German actress Christine Kaufman portraying Helena. Set in biblical time just before the fall and destruction of Pompeii, the story is based on Bulwer Lytton's original novel. Although the story line is similar to Lytton's, director Mario Bonnard and famed co-director Sergio Leone, eventually directing his most famous and acclaimed film *A Fistful of Dollars* in 1963 recreate this new epic tale as a spectacular and suspenseful adventure.

Richard Gertner for *Motion Picture Herald* wrote, *"The film was designed primarily as a showcase for its athletic star, who flexes his muscles with pride in an impressive display of the benefits of physical culture... When it is all over, a thoroughly exhausted spectator can only murmur an admiring 'Wow!'... In his field, Steve Reeves is the undisputed champ!"*

The teaming between director Bonnard and Reeves proved to be productive during filming. Mario believed in Steve and gave him the freedom he needed to be creative with his acting, unlike his co-director Sergio Leone who felt everyone around him needed constant direction. Half way through the filming *Pompeii* Sergio Leone insisted that Reeves stage this one particular fight scene Leone's way and not Steve's. Reeves disagreed. Known within the industry as having a hot temper, Leone blew up and began yelling and pointing his finger in Steve's face. *"I about tore him, and the whole set apart after that incident,"* recalls Steve. *"Leone had a real way of making people angry at times. That particular moment was the maddest I have ever been in my entire life. I just wanted to tear him apart, like I said. That's how angry Sergio Leone made me."*

Up until this time in his movie career, Reeves had never appeared at one of his movie premier's, until now when he did with *Last Days of Pompeii* premiering in Paris. Beginning with *Hercules* all of his other films premiered in countries outside of where he was presently filming. *"I was usually on the other side of the globe shooting a new film when most of my films first opened,"* Reeves recalls.

The Last Days of Pompeii proved to be a greater success both in earnings as well as fan appeal than that of *Goliath and The Barbarians.*

A still from *Last Days of Pompeii* with co-star Christine Kaufman and Reeves, 1960. Courtesy Steve Reeves

During filming of *Pompeii* Reeves experienced an injury that would haunt him physically and emotionally the rest of his life. *"What most people do not know is that I separated my shoulder during this film,"* Steve recalls. During one key action scene when Reeves was performing his own stunt while driving a horse-drawn chariot, he suddenly lost control and crashed into a nearby tree. *"I managed to force my shoulder back into place by myself, but it had settled with a loud thump. Although it ached, I was still able to use my arm,"* Reeves says. The following day, his shoulder received further damage.

During this next stunt scene that required Steve to swim twenty yards under water that had been set aflame with burning diesel fuel Reeves experienced the unexpected. *"I used the breast stroke during this scene but found halfway through the stunt that with each stroke I made I could hear my shoulder ligaments crunching and ripping,"* Steve recalls. *"For obvious reasons, I couldn't surface and couldn't stop so I miraculously forced myself to complete the swim. The damage to my shoulder was massive."*

The Giant of Marathon was Reeves next spectacular drama. Taking place in ancient Greece during the year 490 BC, the mythic story line created by Director Jacques Tourneur centered around the origins of the first Olympic games held in Athens, along with Greece now at odds in war with invading Persian armies. Steve co-stared with french starlet Mylene Demongeot, an ideal teaming for international Reeves fans. Demongeot whose career would end up spanning over six-decades, appearing in seventy-two films received the most fame and adulation in her most noted 1957 film *The Crucible*.

The type casting in *Marathon* suited Reeves very well. *"I very much enjoyed portraying the old-time kinds of roles,"* Reeves says. *"From mythological characters, to cowboys in westerns, to even dramatic modern characters such as Sandokan The Pirate which I later on portrayed. I would have even considered acting in a good comedy, but only if the part was suited for me, and the money was right. The types of roles and films that I do not find of interest are the futuristic films, such as space adventures or science fiction films."*

Mario Bava, who had previously been cinematographer for *Hercules Unchained* once again worked alongside french director

Jacques Tourneur in *Marathon*. The hiring of Bava was a noteworthy choice, as his unique creativity and expertise within lighting and special effects added the layer of success director Toureur was hoping for.

Steve with co-star Mylene Demongeot during the filming of Giant of Marathon.
Courtesy Steve Reeves

For Steve, filming was now more painful than ever. With the constant pain in his left shoulder Reeves decided it would be best not to advertise his injury, afraid this would only jeopardize his career. Confiding only with Aline, the two decided it would be best to keep the matter as quiet as possible. Steve's only remedy for the anguish and pain was the application of hot packs prior to action scenes. With each day of shooting Reeves' only thought was, *"I wondered just how much longer I was going to be able to go on,"* recalls Steve.

The business relationship between Reeves and Joseph E. Levine was at times difficult. There was the on-going dispute as to who made who in the industry? Levine was the individual who right from the start believed in and purchased *Hercules* for U.S release and distribution and backed it with his costly promotional campaign. But without Reeves, who possessed the classic physique and face of Hercules, there would never have been the *Hercules* film for Levine to promote.

In 1975, reporters for *MuscleMag International* magazine quoted Levine as saying, *"As for Steve making me that's not true! It was I who made him. I made him famous."* Reporters noted, that Levine deserved credit, after all he was the guiding master to the film's success.

With his decision now to make his permanent residence in Lucerne, Switzerland, Reeves' regime for health and fitness remained intact. *"I would train real hard for a month and a half to get into great shape before each of my films. Depending on what the role was and called for, I would tailor my training to."* Recalls Steve. Their choice in Lucerne was ideal for Steve, clean fresh air, steep hills and mountain sides for training, and most of all peace and quiet, the one quality in life he always looked to find.

By mid-1960, filming for *Morgan The Pirate* began. Reeves once again co-starred with the Spanish sex bomb Chelo Alonso who portrayed Consuela, an island gypsy bound for romance with Henry Morgan played by Steve Reeves in Joseph E. Levine's third production. Alonso was signed on at the suggestion of Levine who approved of Chelo's appealing performance in *Goliath And The Barbarians..*

The film, along with Reeves's performance were well received by movie reviewers. William Wemeth for *Motion Picture Herald* wrote, *"Steve Reeves, now a familiar and popular marquee name to American audiences, is a robust Morgan. He displays growing ease and assurance as a performer. Overall, the film rates as one of the best in its class."*

Based on the adventurous tale from the mid 1600's, Levine decided to recreate the famed stories of the notorious Welsh buccaneer, Sir Henry Morgan. Andre DeToth was the fourth director in line at creating his movie version of Morgan the pirate. The first three films were *The Black Swan* in 1942 starring Tyrone Power, *Double Crossbones* starring Donald O'Connor in 1951, and 1952's *Black Beard The Pirate* starring Robert Newton. Then in 1960, *The Boy And The Pirates* starring Charles Herbert was made, along with *Pirates Of Tortuga* starring Ken Scott in 1961 trailed side by side with *Morgan The Pirate's* completion in late 1960.

Chelo Alonso starring with Reeves again this time in *Morgan The Pirate*, 1960.
Courtesy Steve Reeves

Upon the release of *Morgan The Pirate* in 1961, Joseph Levine had negotiated with Reeves that if the box office surpassed their initial budget of two million dollars Steve would then receive an extra fifty thousand in royalties. The film did. Unfortunately, Levine backed out of his deal. Levine felt the film had other financial issues in its budgeting and believed that *Morgan The Pirate* had not met its initial budget in pay back. Levine even went as far as to hire three high paid New York lawyers he knew from back home to defend him and his film company *Avco Embassy* Pictures in their case against Reeves. Aline, who acted as Steve's legal representative needed only one hour to double-check and review Steve's contract for the film, knowing that Steve was sure to win the case. After careful review of previous on-site court stenographer tapes, and bound contracts Levine's lawyers had made their final case and decision. Steve recalls of the moment they all sat down in a conference room together, "You should have seen Levine's face when his lawyers delivered the new to him saying, *'Joe, she's got us here. Pay Steve the fifty-thousand dollars he is contracted for.'*

By the early sixties, Reeves popularity and fame had grown so large that his photos would be seen on the cover of hundreds of magazines worldwide now.

Originally Levine wanted to make a third sequel to *Hercules,* but Steve wanted nothing to do with it. *"I felt enough was enough,"* Reeves says. *"I wanted to continue trying different roles, and story lines so that I could further my career."* In 1965 at the suggestion of Steve, Levine eventually signed on Gordon Scott instead as his lead character in *Hercules And The Princess Of Troy.* Scott, who starred the 1959 film *Tarzan's Greatest Adventures* tried his shot at capitalizing on the money-making *Hercules* role, fully knowing that his Hollywood friend Reeves had already capitalized and conquered that role, a thousand time over. Levine even went as far as making a *Hercules* television mini-series based on the original mega-film. The idea flopped, and the pilot never sold. Levine did go on to a lucrative career with other big movie hits such as 1967's *The Graduate* starring Dustin Hoffman, and *A Bridge Too Far* 1967 starring James Caan and Sean Connery.

In mid-1959, only months before departing for Ischia, a small village north of Capri Steve was interviewed by a *TIME* magazine reporter saying, *"All I need now is the right director. Possibly someone like Joshua Logan, Elia Kazan, or even John Lord along with the right script and I'll be off and running."*

By 1960, Steve began filming his second contracted film with Joseph E. Levine, this time under the direction of American director Arthur Lubin. In its third remake, originally starring Douglas Fairbanks, Sr. *The Thief Of Baghdad* was a popular fantasy classic filmed primarily in Tunisia. The tale was based on the adventures of the Arabian Knights. Steve played the main character Karim, a clever but charming thief who after stealing the clothes of a prince finds himself unexpectedly at the altar to wed the sultan's daughter, Amina played by Giorgia Moll who previously co-starred alongside Reeves two years earlier in Riccardo Freda's *The White Warrior*.

Director Arthur Lubin, who had previously directed comedy in the 1950's television series *Francis The Talking Mule* was chosen to direct Levine's next big hit. Levine, along with supporting producers felt Arthur Lubin would be the ideal director for the whimsical and magical tale. *The Thief Of Baghdad's* budget was enormous for this time in movie making standards, two million dollars was spent on sets designs, special effects and wardrobes alone. *"The costumes were unbelievable,"* Reeves recalls. *"They were tailored with such expertise that you didn't want to give them back. That's how perfect they were."* The only film close in budget and design was that of Levine's previous production of *Morgan The Pirate*. Although the team of Levine and Reeves reached unprecedented success at the box office, unfortunately the two were unable to work together any more. While in Rome on vacation, just weeks after the completion of *Baghdad* Steve and Aline stopped by the Excelsior Hotel where Levine was staying. As Steve retells the story, Levine had wanted to change again another detail in his negotiations with the film. *"I have always contracted that my name would appear a minimum of seventy-five percent of the height of the title of the film,"* Steve says. *"And with the understanding that nobody's name would appear more than fifty percent of the title. Well, Levine insisted that his name match my name in size."* The contract was iron clad and the producer could not change the negotiation. *"Levine got so angry at me that he took his dinner plate threw it up into the air hitting the ceiling and chandelier. Well food splattered everywhere, we just turned around and left."* Steve says. It would be several years before the two would ever speak to each other again.

From a more positive standpoint, reviews for *The Thief Of Baghdad* were very supportive. The *St. Louis Post Dispatch* wrote, *"I daresay there is a generation growing up today which believes in Steve Reeves the same way we used to believe in Douglas Fairbanks..."* And Marjory Adams for *Boston Herald Traveler* said, *"The theatre is mobbed with Reeves enthusiasts who want to see his latest, and who appear to enjoy each astounding whimsy and bit of fantasy...Karim wins his princess, and the audience sits still, hoping to see the picture all over again."*

From beginning to end, production was a huge success. Although for Reeves, language barriers and foreign customs remained a constant challenge for him. Working abroad, year after year was beginning to wear on Steve. For the most part, healthy food and nutrition was usually not a problem to find, but there were times when adaptation was needed. "One day, in the early part of filming *Baghdad* we all broke for lunch." Reeves recalls. *"The luncheon was being served in this very large room that you would enter by means of this grand stairwell. Far away it looked as though there was a very large salad prepared for us, garnished heavily in caviar that awaited us. But when we got closer to serve ourselves the caviar flew away. Flies! From then on, all I ate and drank while there in Tunisia was bread, cheese, canned tuna and beer."* laughs Steve.

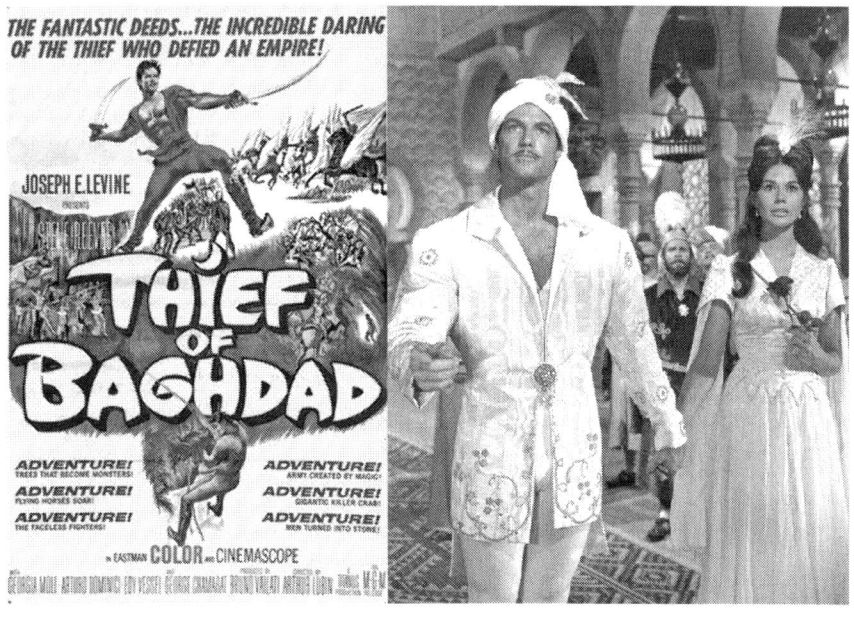

Steve starring in The Thief Of Baghdad, as seen here with co-star Giorgia Moll, 1960. Courtesy Steve Reeves

The Trojan Horse was Reeves next mythic movie. It the film Steve portrays the ancient Spartan warrior Aeneas in the Greek saga between the Trojans and the Spartans. Starring opposite Reeves was co-star John Drew Barrymore, Jr. as Ulysses. John was member of the Barrymore family of actors, whose father was John Barrymore and daughter Drew went on to act primarily in television playing bit roles in both *Gunsmoke* and *Rawhide*. Reeves recalls, *"John was really just starting out. He was living over there in Rome at the time and landed the part. He had a very famous name in the industry, and that was about it."* When asked about socializing or partying with Barrymore and the other cast members during this time Steve responded, *"I never went out partying with any of them. At the end of the day, I would go straight home. I never hung around to do this or that. When filming was all done I wanted to be alone, not out partying or socializing."*

Rewritten from the original story *Helen of Troy*, the film's second co-star played by Edy Vessel portrayed Helen, who's character is captured by the Trojan army in hopes that the Spartans will surrender their protected city of Troy for her safe return. Vessel had previously worked with Reeves co-starring with Giorgia Moll the year before in *The Thief Of Baghdad*. Producer's were very pleased with Edy's performance in *Baghdad* and felt her co-starring with Reeves in *The Trojan Horse* would prove to be a profitable decision.

In April of 1962, *The Trojan Horse* was released to theatres in both Italy and Yugoslavia. For his role of Aeneas, Reeves received a salary of one-hundred and seventy-five thousand dollars. By now Aline had helped secure sound investments for Steve's retirement, primarily through Swiss bank investments. Up until 1962, anyone residing in Europe for at least eighteen months did not have to pay taxes on foreign earnings. But by 1962, any U.S citizens working in Europe had to pay under newly amended U.S. tax laws. Each year now, Reeves' goal of retiring by age forty-five seemed more of a reality.

In an action-packed scene Reeves wields his sword against his enemies in *The Trojan Horse*, 1961. Courtesy Joe Sciambra

Filmed in Yugoslavia, *The Trojan Horse* was a repeat for Reeves in genre. With its Romanesque flair in set designs and props, Director Giorgio Ferroni provided a very significant and unique detail to the film, a real life thirty-foot tall wooden replica of the actual wooden horse used during the battle of Troy in 1200 BC. The recreation was constructed so heavily and well-made that camera crews were able to set up inside the replica for added camera angles. On the flip side of production, Ferroni was a very emotional and outspoken director. At times during filming he would get so upset over how a scene was not playing out the way he wanted it to, Ferroni would simply walk off the set either go for a walk or even go fishing for thirty minutes or so just to calm his nerves.

With Joseph E. Levine now out of the picture, Steve still managed to hold onto his salary earnings. Unfortunately for Reeves, his films did lack the heavy hitting producers to budget his films. Beginning with *The Trojan Horse,* Steve's remaining five films would begin to greatly decline. His choice in roles were plainly repeats of his previous films; biblical hero, Roman warrior, and swashbuckling pirate. Regardless of what critics believed, Reeves' popularity with fans did remain at an all-time high. But by 1963, his movies were now beginning a gradual descent into mediocrity.

In late 1961, production began with the filming of *Duel of The Titans*. American actor Gordon Scott portrayed Remos co-starring alongside Reeves who played Romulus in the original biblical storyline. Taken place in the year 733 BC, the film covers the founding of Rome, weaving the story of Romulus and Remos, twin brothers abandoned along the Nile river, who are eventually found and cared for by a she-wolf until the age of one, when a hunter discovers the two infants in the wolf's den.

Originally, *Titanus* Productions wanted Steve to play both parts of Romulos and Remos, with the aid of special effects. This notion was quickly canned. At the suggestion of Reeves, Gordon Scott was signed on to play opposite Reeves as Remos. Gordon had previously known Steve through the bodybuilding circuit back in California, and like Reeves had begun his own acting career back in 1955 starring in first b&w film RKO Pictures *Tarzan's Hidden Jungle*. Scott went on to film five more Tarzan films, and starred in a total of twenty-six films throughout his career.

The primary issue *Titanus* had with Scott was the salary he was asking for. At the time, Gordon Scott's agent was also Steve's agent, his girlfriend Aline. *Titanus* was not even sold on the fact that they even wanted Scott for the part, much less pay him the fifty-thousand U.S dollars Aline was attempting to contract him for. Fully aware of Scott's recent success as *Tarzan*, *Titanus* along with producers once again declined their offer. That's when Reeves stepped in. Steve recalls saying *"I told them, look. If Gordon goes, I go! He's the only guy I want to play this part, and I know he can do it."* Although the teaming of Scott and Reeves was well received by movie goers, working alongside Gordon did not. Scott's daily habit of being late every morning for filming, do to his staying up all night partying became a constant battle not only with Reeves, but with the director Sergio Corbucci.

As for the female lead part, blond, blue-eyed Italian beauty Virna Lisi was chosen to play Julia. The role was actually added into the script, derived from the original biblical story-line so as to lighten the amount of violence within the film. Critics were all for the addition of Julia, one reviewer wrote, *"The physically immaculate Lisi admirably complements the equally immaculate Reeves and Scott."* Lisi would go on to co-star with Anthony Quinn in *The Twenty Fifth Hour* starring Anthony Quinn, and *Assault On A Queen* co-starring Frank Sinatra. In total Virna would appear in seventy-five films throughout her career.

Director Corbucci had previously worked with Reeves two years earlier, when he co-wrote *The Last Days Of Pompeii* in collaboration with director Sergio Leone. Steve found Corbucci a delight to work with, contrary to that of Sergio Leone and fondly remembers Corbucci as a very enjoyable and funny person.

Fans for both Scott and Reeves knew what to expect in advertisements for the film upon its release to theaters in 1962. *'Hercules vs Tarzan! Come See The Main Event!'* read many of the large movie poster ads. Producers desperately tried to pick-up where Joseph E. Levine had left off with his Reeves films. Still, *Titans* did not receive the earnings it had hoped to cash in on, even with the clever pairing of Reeves and Scott.

A 1961 Japanese movie poster for *Duel Of The Titans*. Steve poses during a scene with co-star Virna Lisi. Courtesy Steve Reeves

The cast did receive moderate attention from critics with Robert Salmaggi for the *New York Herald Tribune* writing, *"Figure it this way. Instead of just one mountain of muscle to thrill that faithful clique of movie fans, action-lovers, etc., why not two... to double the pleasure, as they say, and thereby coin a double mint at the box office."* Mint, or no mint, fans still remained faithful to Reeves even with his redundant choice in character and film.

The Avenger, The Legend Of Aeneas was the second of three 1962 films Reeves filmed and starred in. The film was also released in some countries under the title *The Last Glory of Troy*. Shot and released in black and white, *The Avenger* ironically, turned out to be a sequel to Giorgio Ferroni's *The Trojan Horse*. Opening in Paris theatres in April 1964, *Avenger* turned out to be almost identical to its predecessor *The Trojan Horse*. Steve said of the two films, *"Both The Trojan Horse and The Avenger were very identical films for me to star in. Basically, they both had the same *story line, similar scripts, scenes and even moods. The two seemed inseparable."*

Reeves plays the part of Aeneas, a Trojan soldier who travels to Italy where he ultimately becomes the leader of the Roman Empire. The story line covers Aeneas' journey from Troy to Italy, and finally into victorious battle against the Latins, leading escaped survivors of the Trojan war to their new land of Italy. The screenplay co-written by the film's producer Albert Band was derived from the original epic poem written by Virgil, *The Aeneid* in 29 BC.

Filmed in Yugoslavia, *The Avenger* was directed by the Italian Giorgio Venturini. Production went smoothly as companies were able to negotiate with the Yugoslavian government to contract building space, and military personnel and equipment for filming. *"It worked out great,"* recalls Reeves. *"They chose Yugoslavia, primarily for its reduction in production costs, cutting expenses down to five-hundred thousand. And if we filmed it back here in the states, the film would have cost easily two-million to make. The European film companies really knew how to budget their films."*

The Avenger co-starring Carla Marlier seen here with Reeves on location in Yugoslavia, 1962. A French movie poster edition of *The Avenger, The Legend Of Aeneas.* Courtesy Steve Reeves

Albert Band who co-wrote the screenplay was already an accomplished American screenwriter, producer and director. Band and his team of technicians decided to bring the two films *The Trojan Horse* and *The Avenger* into one film, through this sequel. Albert purposely spliced actual footage from *The Trojan Horse* into *The Avenger* to depict flashbacks of Aeneas during the war on Troy. A creative and clever marketing scheme not only for the story line, but for Steve Reeves fans getting double their money while watching their hero once again up on the silver screen.

The Avenger opened in Paris in April 1964 almost simultaneously with Reeves next film, *The Slave, Son Of Spartacus.*

Box Office review wrote, *"Steve Reeves, the much-publicized Hercules of global screen status, essays yet another*

portrayal in this competently enough produced and directed historical spectacle... Reeves does well indeed..."

The appeal of Steve Reeves remained high and opportunities for future roles continued to role in. English director Terrance Young, who was part of the casting crew for a new British film titled *Dr. No,* the first James Bond 007 film was looking for the right actor to portray the secret double agent. The only drawback for Reeves was the fifty-thousand-dollar salary, a quarter of what Reeves was now earning per film. Unknowingly, Steve turned down Terrence Young's movie deal. Years later, following the huge success of *Dr. No* Reeves said, *"How was I to know that the film would take off the way it did and make millions?"*

After his turning down Young's offer for *Dr No,* Steve landed the role of Randus, a roman centurion spy in *The Slave, Son Of Spartacus* shot on location in Cairo, Egypt in late of 1962.

Director Sergio Corbucci who had previously directed Reeves in *Duel Of The Titans* the year before once again collaborated with Steve in the film derived from Stanley Kubrick's 1960 film *Spartacus* starring Kirk Douglas.

Set in 73 BC, *The Slave* opens up with Julius Caesar, played by Claudio Gora devising a secret mission for Randus played by Reeves to travel in secrecy to Lydia in hopes of finding out how Vetius, played by Jacques Sernas is attempting to overthrow and possibly kill Julius Ceasar. In his attempt, Randus is captured and enslaved but eventually leads a successful revolt against Vetius.

Reeves experience while on location in Egypt turned out to be a spiritual fulfillment. In an interview by John Little for *MuscleMag International* magazine Reeves said, *"I loved Egypt. Something was very powerful and moving there for me. It was indescribable."* Years later, Reeves again referred to this experience in saying, *"For me, I felt as though I had lived the life of a very high-ranking king there, or an official. It was a very positive experience for me."*

Reeves on horseback during the filming of *The Slave, Son Of Spartacus* shot on location in Egypt, 1962. Courtesy Steve Reeves

With each new film now, critics were less kind to the one-time Mr. Universe. Stephen Flacassier wrote in his book *Muscle, Myths & Movies, "In The Trojan Horse, we got to see very little of his (Reeves) build and there's even less in The Avenger,"* Flacassier said. *"Like most sex symbols who try and go legit, Reeves cut down on the amount of flesh seen with each movie but made sure there was one scene to keep his old fans happy. Reeves build was beginning to slip a little..."*

The Slave opened in theatres January 1964 followed by standard reviews. For *Motion Picture Herald* Raymond Levy wrote, *"It is a screenplay that might have been, and probably was, created for the muscular righteousness - In-action type of role now so thoroughly established by the screen's king of the strong-men. Reeves is believable to his many admirers who delight in watching him in that kind of a performance."*

One week before the completion of *The Slave* Steve received unfortunate news from back home. Through *Telegram*, Goldie wrote to Steve informing him that his step-father Earl, who had been suffering from emphysema for many years now due to heavy smoking, had recently died. The day after the final day of shooting, Reeves flew back to Oregon in time to attend Earl's funeral and to console his mother.

By the spring of 1963, good news soon followed. Nearly seven years since his divorce from Sandra Smith, Reeves proposed to Aline while on break between movies. This time his courtship was with a thirty-year old Princess belonging to the honorable Radziwill family, to whom Jacqueline Onassis was related. Aline Czarjarwicz would marry Steve, now thirty-seven years of age at St. Marco's church in Lucerne, Switzerland on June 24th., 1963. Immediately following ceremonies, Steve and Aline flew to Majorca, Spain where they spent their honeymoon.

By mid-July, Reeves latest contracted film *Sandokan The Great* was now ready to begin filming. Based on Emilio Salgari's novel *The Tiger Of Mompracem* Steve played the role of Sandokan, a sultan's son who turns jungle guerrilla to free his father and the woman he loves, Mary Ann played by co-star Genevieve Grad from the ruthless tyrants of Borneo.

Mr. & Mrs. Steve and Aline Reeves wed on June 24th, 1963 in Lucerne, Switzerland. Courtesy Steve Reeves

Sandokan The Great was a two-part sequel starring Steve Reeves and Genevieve Grad in 1963. Courtesy Steve Reeves

While on location in Ceylon, Sri Lanka actors were required to wear scuba suits from the waist down while filming in the river scenes so as to protect themselves from leaches. *"The problem was we still never knew what else was crawling around our legs,"* Steve recalls. *"There were things always squirming and sliding around you, but you could never see what it was due to the muddy waters."*

Filmed in 1963 *Sandokan The Great* was the first, of a two-part film series directed by Umberto Lenzi. Upon its release June 2nd, 1966 in Paris, the film would also be released under the title *The Shortest Day* in various other countries in part do to international marketing.

Sandokan The Great received strong praise internationally, much so than here in the U.S. Asian and Southern Pacific regions of the world were where the *Sandokan* films really took off. *"They could have been a lot better than they were,"* Reeves says. *"Between the film's lower than average budget, and a shooting schedule that rushed filming do to our extensive travel schedule between Spain and Greece the film's outcome and quality were drastically effected."*

Upon the *Sandokan's* completion, Steve received a phone call from his less than friendly producer Sergio Leone offering Reeves a new film idea. For several years, Leone had admired Japanese director Akiro Kurosawa and his film *Yojimbo* and felt he could adapt the story line to a cowboy western, the same way director John Sturges had in his 1960 adaptation of Kurosawa's *The Seven Samurai* in *The Magnificent Seven* starring Yul Brenner and Steve McQueen.

Reeves had always remained hopeful of starring in a western, and with this in mind read the script. *"I remained reluctant with Leone's idea for one reason,"* Reeves recalls. *"I remember asking myself, what do Italians know about cowboys, and the old west?"* It wasn't until reading halfway through the script that Reeves declined. *"I was immediately turned off by the brutality and excessive, uncalled for violence in the the story,"* Steve says. *"I felt it would not be accepted, at that time, by American audiences."* Within months of Steve's refusal Leone signed on a young American actor by the name of Clint Eastwood and titled the film *A Fistful of Dollars*. What Leone's film did for Eastwood, is what Levine's *Hercules* had done for Reeves, catapulted the two young American actors into movie stardom. *"I probably made a big mistake,"* Reeves says. *"But at the time, I thought I was doing the right thing. I'm not saying what happened to Clint Eastwood would have happened to me, but it could have."*

Once again, under the direction of Umberto Lenzi, the sequel to *Sandokan The Great* titled, *Pirates Of The Seven Seas* began filming. Sharing similar characters and plot, Lenzi's script was adapted from Emilio Salgari's second book *The Pirates of Malaya*.

Crew members from *Sandokan, Pirates Of The Seven Seas* joke with Reeves between takes. Courtesy Milton Moore

The story takes place in Bombay, in the year 1897. The English led by Lord Burke co-starring Mimmo Palmara are at war with *Sandokan*, played by Reeves. Palmara portrays a vengeful captain along with his gang pirates aim at controlling the oceans of the South Pacific, while hoping to kill off Sandokan and his army of men. Mimmo Palmara who was a new cast member to Umberto's second Sandokan film had already acted alongside Reeves in four of his previous films; *Hercules, Hercules Unchained, The Last Days Of Pompeii, The Trojan Horse,* and would eventually act alongside Steve in his last film *A Long Ride From Hell*.

Two years after the completion of *Pirates Of The Seven Seas* Reeves attempted to star in his first documentary film *The Life Story Of Angel Peralta* based on the life story of Spain's famed bull fighter. In the fall of 1965 Reeves underwent two months of intense training in Seville, Spain with rejoneador masters learning the time-honored sport. Unfortunately, only weeks before filming production was halted. Do to the films controversial subject matter, producers felt the documentary would not receive the kind of financial attention and support it needed beyond the movie theatres of Spain and Portugal.

For the next three years, while still residing in Switzerland, Steve would remain in hiatus. He still had one more life-long goal to achieve in starring in films, and this was to make a cowboy western.

Since the early 1960's Steve had been searching for an ideal story line to base his last and final film on prior to retirement. Reading well over one-hundred western themed books from such novelists as Louis L'Amour, Zane Gray and Gordon Sheriff, Reeves eventually chose the novel *Judas Gun* by Gordon Sheriff. Previous novels of Gordon's that were also made into films were *Rio Bravo* and *The Last Train From Gun Hill*. After tracking down Gordon in the U.S, Steve was able to purchase the rights to his book for twenty-thousand dollars in early 1968.

Aside from starring in *A Long Ride,* Steve was also co-producer, technical director and co-screen writer for the script. The film was based on the notorious Yuma Arizona State Penitentiary, and its set design was replicated by Reeves upon conducting an extensive study of the current state landmark and museum. *"I flew back to the U.S from Switzerland to study the entire prison and grounds in person."* Reeves recalls. *"I took countless photos while *there, and even drew a series of sketches, complete with measurements outlining the entire facility."* By late March, film and production crews assembled in the small coastal town of Almeria in southern Spain to begin filming.

In *A Long Ride From Hell,* Steve played the role of Mike Sturges, the eldest son of horse ranchers who as a result of a mix up with train robbers has been beaten up, arrested and thrown in jail. After making friends on the inside Sturges puts together a plan that will help break them all out of prison. Playing opposite Reeves, is Wayde Preston as Bart Meyner, a ranch friend who turns against Sturges and is the one responsible for his arrest. Previously starring in the late 1950s television series *Colt 45,* Preston was chosen for the part due to similar previous roles. *"I knew Wayde would play a great rival to me,"* Steve recalls. *"Plus, he was good looking, great in action westerns, and was an excellent horseman."*

Originally, Reeves hoped for Riccardo Freda to direct the film, but *BRC* Films and producers were not willing to pay Freda's undisclosed asking price. Instead Alex Burks (a.k.a. Camillo Bazzoni) filled the bill. Although reluctant with their choice, Reeves found he worked well with Burks.

To look the role physically of an authentic cowboy, Steve had to trim his body weight down. *"I needed to lose about fifteen pounds,"* Reeves said, *"which would put me at around 185 pounds. That way it would give me a taller, leaner look for the film."*

Upon the completion of *A Long Ride From Hell* in late spring of 1968, Steve's movie career came to a roaring halt. Movie reviewers for his last film were not exactly what producer's at BRC or Reeves were hoping for. Although the film did receive its initial production costs back, the film came in last with ticket sales in comparison to Reeves previous international block buster hits.

Reeves starring in his last film *A Long Ride From Hell* prior to his retirement at age forty-three, 1969. Courtesy Steve Reeves

In a *Muscle & Fitness* magazine article Steve said, *"I never planned to remain in the movies all my life. I was never enthralled with being an actor from the beginning. But what I did enjoy was the challenge that went along with it. Movies were a means to an end for me. I enjoyed making films, but like I have said, it was a very stressful and tiring career choice for me. I didn't have to quit. I had plenty of offers every year but the pain in my shoulder which I had been battling with for too long just wasn't worth it. I could no longer fake it. Every action scene I did only made it worse. I wasn't about to do Lawrence Olivier type movies my thing was action-adventure. It was inevitable that a new trend in public tastes would come along shortly, and it did."*

One thing did remain certain with Reeves, the overwhelming attraction and admiration he received from fans worldwide through his talents and efforts in film. Through the mid-1950s and up until 1970, upon the release of *A Long Ride from Hell* Steve Reeves had more fans within the bodybuilding circuit and movie world than any other bodybuilder turned actor had up until that time. This alone secured Reeves a permanent place in Hollywood's record books.

Though his movie making days were now over, the amazing impact Steve Reeves had in Hollywood would remain for decades.

For Reeves his goal of retirement had finally been reached.

Reeves standing proudly behind his bodybuilding trophies at his Valley Center horse ranch. Courtesy Steve Reeves

CHAPTER FOURTEEN

Cowboy Redux

"I am seriously considering moving to a remote area of Australia where no one can bother or find me. I just want my privacy, peace, and quiet."

- Steve Reeves, *Muscle Training Illustrated* magazine 1970

Having worked for years to achieve stardom, how could Reeves just walk away and not look back? Why would a star at the top of his profession simply stop making films? These are questions that many of his fans and admirers have wondered about him over the years.

One day while we were unloading hay in a stable, Reeves explained this to me. *"My body has always remained first in life."* Steve said as we hauled bails from his truck. *"It has always been that way, well before any career, movie contract or all the money in the world. After A Long Ride From Hell, I knew that my body was not up for it any more. I was more than happy to leave the film business, and at that point I had made enough money so that I could live off my investments for the rest of my life. I had always said that I would retire by age forty-five but ended my career by age forty-four, thankfully."*

In early 1969, after *A Long Ride From Hell* was still showing a theatre's throughout Europe and the U.S, Reeves began experiencing a strange and massive hunger within in nutritional diet, particularly craving bread and cheese. Aline insisted that he get a checkup at the doctor's office in Rome, a completely foreign notion for him since he had not had a physical since his discharge in 1946 from the military.

So, Steve and Aline flew to Rome for the best medical care they knew of outside Switzerland, and X-rays revealed that Reeves had a severe duodenal stomach ulcer. *A Long Ride From Hell* had been so stressful for Steve, and now being diagnosed with a severe ulcer only reinforced his decision to now stop making films. The doctors in Italy wanted him to stay at the hospital for several more days until he was strong enough to go home, but Reeves insisted on being released at once. Reluctantly, the doctors agreed on the condition that he stay in bed for six weeks and follow a very bland diet.

"I think again, intuition helped me," Reeves recalled years later during an interview with Armand Tanny. *"I was able to cure myself in my own way. You see, I had a terrible craving for Jell-0, and so I ate bowls of it, thickened with plain Knox gelatin every day. Within two months, the symptoms had disappeared. Several months later, out of curiosity, I went back for X-rays, and the doctors told me that not only was I completely cured, that there was no sign of scarring. I strongly believe to this day that the gelatin cured me. I had a need for it, and for its pure protein."*

Once again, he followed his intuition without question. *"I believe instinct and intuition can show you the way,"* Reeves says.

"It is more than believing. I didn't consciously think gelatin was going to cure me. It was just something I felt I had to have. I guess it was nature's way of telling me, here is your cure.'"

When reflecting on his film career, a business he found stressful and except for the money and travel, which are *"unappealing"* Reeves says, he left with only one regret.

"If I were to go back and do it all over again, the one thing I would do differently is pay more attention to how the director worked and performed his job," Steve says. *"Instead, I just concentrated on what they were telling me to do, and simply starred in the movie. Now, as I look back over my career, I really think I would have preferred to be a good director, or even a good camera man instead of a movie star. Don't get me wrong, I very much enjoyed the satisfaction of having the public enjoy my movies and believing in me. When you're the lead actor of a film, everything is highly expected of you. In addition, directors and camera men did not have to shave, they could stay up all night long and show up to work the next day ten minutes before shooting began, and with circles under their eyes. But I would have to go to bed by nine every night just to get a good night's sleep and to look rested. I had to be on the set hours before the director and camera men did for make-up and such. I couldn't stand it."*

Having lived in Lucerne, Switzerland for ten years now, Reeves and Aline were eligible for Swiss citizenship, but Steve was beginning to grow restless living in Europe. He wanted to return to the surroundings of his early years of both ranch life and horses. Although initially reluctant to leave the cosmopolitan lifestyle of Europe, Aline was willing to give it a try. In 1970, they decided to move back to their California property Steve had purchased with his earnings from *Hercules* in 1957, a place they named *La Hacienda Del Sol*. There, Reeves began raising Morgan horses.

Ranch life suited Steve, a connection with nature harmonized him in a way nothing else had since his childhood. Reeves is an extremely private individual and found contentment with his wife Aline on the farm.

"We read a lot. We laugh. We joke. We argue sometimes. We travel. We have nice friends. I guess we live like all married people do," Aline said in a 1983 *Muscle & Fitness* magazine interview. *"He's a knockout, but physical beauty isn't all. I think what captured the screen public was the soul of the man. He doesn't blow his own horn. He has had all the acclaim and practically every award there is both in physical fitness and motion pictures, but I think he finds most rewarding the fact that he has been an inspiration to people."*

The next nineteen years were to be a period of personal fulfillment, public recognition and private pain for Reeves.

Still maintaining an impressive physique, Reeves was an elder statesman for the sport of bodybuilding. On February 9, 1978 at age fifty-four, Reeves was awarded *The President's Council on Physical Fitness and Sports Award* in recognition of his outstanding and significant contributions to the sport of bodybuilding and fitness over the years.

In the following years Steve Reeves was to be honored nationally, numerous times. In 1981 Rudy Riska, manager of *The Downtown Athletic Club* in Manhattan, called Reeves to tell him about a new award the club had just sponsored. *The Steve Reeves Award* was to be given each year to an athlete who made a notable contribution to both sports and fitness during his or her lifetime.

Steve with wife Aline at their Valley Center horse ranch, 1985. Courtesy Steve Reeves

"I choose Steve Reeves as the person for which the award was to be named," Riska said. *"Steve was not only a pioneer within the sport of bodybuilding but was also one of the very few who never took steroids in order to compete."*

The first recipient was Buster Crabbe, a 1932 Olympic gold medal swimmer who later gained Hollywood fame starring as *Flash Gordon* in 1935, and *Buck Rogers in 1938* as well as various other film and television roles. The following years, fitness legend Jack LaLanne received the honor. Among other honorees were Frank Gifford in 1984, Julius Erving, 1987, Tom Seaver, 1988, and Shannon Miller in 1992.

Obviously, Reeves's passion for bodybuilding and fitness had not dimmed over the years, but increasingly Steve was finding it difficult to maintain his standard routine. Since his shoulder accident during the filming of *Last Days Of Pompeii,* Steve had lost full range of motion in his left arm and shoulder. He decided to have surgery, although the doctors were uncertain of the prognosis since nearly twenty years had passed since the accident. Undeterred, Reeves underwent surgery and his recovery was successful, as far as the relief from pain. As for the range of motion in his shoulder only half was recovered.

Another project now captured Steve's attention, he began writing his first book and detailing an innovation in the fitness field he devised early in 1977 called power walking.

In the introduction of his 1982 book *Power Walking* published by Bobs-Merrill Press, Steve wrote, *"Actually my discovery of power walking as an ideal form of exercise came about rather casually during a time when I was training my Morgan horses. One day in the spring of 1977, I was leading a thirty-mile trail ride from the town of Anza, California through the mountains and down Coyote Canyon to a horse camp in Borrego*

Springs. I decided for the sake of the relatively unconditioned riders and their mounts to conduct this ride cavalry style: you dismount and walk beside your horse for ten minutes out of each hour. When I called the first halt and got off by horse and started to walk beside him I found to my surprise that I had trained him to walk so fast that It was nearly impossible to keep up with him.

"I learned that by lengthening my stride and picking up my pace while swinging my arms in rhythm and taking deeper breaths, I was able to keep up with my horse. I also observed that at the end of the ten-minute walk my horse and I had left the other riders and their mounts far behind. As I stood there waiting there to catch up 1 reviewed in my mind what I had experienced in that ten-minute walk. I had been breathing more deeply thus increasing my oxygen intake and my heartbeat had quickened considerably and remained accelerated. It was a great aerobic exercise. For weeks I spent several hours almost daily experimenting with power walking to improve its effectiveness as a conditioning technique. Power walking was the answer to my prayers."

Reeves new publication placed him once again back into the lime light, establishing Steve once again as a true pioneer within the field of physical fitness and exercise. *Power Walking* earned positive reviews and went back to press five times. In 1983 Steve even appeared on ABC's *Good Morning America* to promote his new revolutionary fitness approach and new book.

Grounded, fit, and still idolized by hundreds of thousands of fans worldwide, in 1985 Reeves was hit with the first, of two traumatic losses.

On April 13, 1984 at the age of seventy-nine, Steve's mother Goldie died of a stroke while on her ranch in Cave Junction, Oregon. His only mother lifelong supporter, the woman who had absolutely believed in his destiny from the time he was a young teenager lifting weights in their Oakland garage was now gone. One-week later Goldie was buried at The Cave Junction Cemetery with Steve, Aline, and numerous friends in attendance.

In no small measure, much of Steve's success and determination can be credited to his upbringing from Goldie, a woman of uncommon strength. Reeves recalls of a phrase his mother would continually say to him, *"Many times when I would discuss a new goal of mine to my mother and ask her for her advice on my decision, she would always say to me, 'Steve, if you think you can do it, then do it!'"* he recalls. *"Just make sure you accomplish whatever you set your mind to doing."*

Four years later, on July fourth two days after Reeves left for a two-week vacation back to his home state of Montana, Aline also experienced a sudden stroke.

Steve got word on the sixth and immediately drove non-stop back to Valley Center reaching Palomar Hospital twenty-hours later where he found Aline resting in stable condition. By Saturday, the doctors were confident enough to release her. While dressing for the return trip home, Aline experienced a second stroke and was immediately put into intensive care. Later that night on Sunday, July twenty-third Aline suffered a third stroke and passed on early the next morning. She was fifty-seven years old. Her burial three days later, on July twenty-six at the El Camino Memorial Park cemetery just a few miles outside La Jolla left Steve, her only husband of twenty-six years speechless.

In the following months, Reeves began to lose faith in himself experiencing extreme depression. For the first time in his life, Steve stopped all physical training and exercise. He had always been known as an extremely private person and with Aline's death occurring so soon after his mother's death caused him to retreat even further.

In 1993, at sixty-seven years old Reeves was to begin a new chapter in his life. A neighbor of many years, Deborah Englehorn, thirty-nine years of age often stopped by the ranch to say hello. The divorced mother of two (son Lynx and daughter Naomi) shared with Reeves a love of horses, ranch life and the great outdoors and soon she was to rekindle Steve's interest in life.

With Deborah at his side, once again Reeves had begun to make occasional appearances at fitness conventions, film festivals and bodybuilding competitions often as the keynote speaker and honored guest both here in the States, as well in Europe.

Steve with girlfriend Deborah during a vacation back to Montana, 1994.
Courtesy Steve Reeves

Author Christopher LeClaire with Mr. America - George Eiferman, Steve Reeves and famed photographer Russ Warner enjoy a fourth of July party at Reeves horse ranch in 1994. Photo taken by Deborah Englehorn

Today, a typical day for Steve begins at six o'clock in the morning. For breakfast he has the same meal almost every day. *"I have a tall glass of orange juice freshly squeezed from oranges that I pick from my own trees here on the ranch, a banana, and some bee pollen tablets along with my various vitamins,"* Reeves says. *"That gives me the energy I need."*

After a brisk power walk, Steve goes to his home gym, a converted section of his garage he fashioned after his original homestead back in East Oakland where he works out between thirty to forty-five minutes, three days a week.

Ranch chores are scheduled for mid-mornings before the desert sun is at its highest. He then eats lunch at high noon and always takes a nap by one in the afternoon for about two hours.

By three-thirty, Steve gets up and often-times goes horseback riding for an hour or two, showers and has dinner by five-thirty ending the day by watching the nightly news followed by one of his favorite television sitcoms.

The discipline that forged Reeeves' life through three careers continues to shape his days today.

Reeves with the author Christopher LeClaire at Reeves Valley Center horse ranch, 1993. Photo taken by Deborah Englehorn

CHAPTER FIFTEEN

Sunrise

"My philosophy of life is one of adaptation, to be able to function regardless of your means in life. Don't have too many material demands in life and try to lead a balanced life without being fanatical in any way."

- Steve Reeves, Valley Center, CA. 1999

    The early morning was like any other day on the ranch. The air was cool, not yet affected by the rising sun just now making its way over the distant Palomar Mountains. This was the ideal time for riding.

    With the chores complete, Steve and I focused on preparing the two Morgan's. While Reeves rigged his favorite horse Torrey, I began preparing my saddle for Monte, the primary horse I rode during my stays there at the ranch for both summers.

In the tack room, Reeves took his saddle from one of the rests the very same one Steve told me that he had used while filming *A Long Ride From Hell* back in 1968. As we fit the bridal bits and buckle the saddle girth straps our horses begin to become edgy and skittish with the knowledge that soon we would all be cantering off into the nearby mountain sides.

We depart from the stables. With Reeves in the lead, we ride down a narrow dirt trail and through an abandoned orchard road that leads up to a nearby hillside.

Steve's equestrian skills are evident, he rides his horse with the expertise of a champion horseman, the ease of a seasoned cowboy. He demonstrated great poise and confidence as we cantered through the low sage brush of the semi desert terrain. We traveled for a while in silence, a stillness broken only when Steve would sing a line or two from an old trail song he liked. Laughing at times, Reeves would yell back to me saying, *"Chris sing along, you must know that tune?"* When the terrain allowed, we would bring the horses abreast and chat. Even while talking, Steve was always aware of his surroundings, alert for places a horse might catch a hoof or unexpected hazards.

As we reached the main ridge, the valley below us went on for miles. I scanned the view for several moments then glanced over at Reeves. He sat looking out with his cowboy hat titled back. He gazed across his hometown valley and out to the distant Palomar mountains, slightly smiling that split his suntanned face. Steve looked alive and young at a place you could tell he truly felt at one with and appreciated. *"This is a great place, isn't it Chris?"* Reeves said to me.

I realized at that moment that Reeves had learned a very important element in life. This man who earned global success and recognition in ways very few will ever experience, knew a key answer in life and this was to celebrate our existence as simple as possible, through one's connection with nature.

A *Muscle & Fitness* tribute to Steve Reeves. Courtesy Joe Weider

CHAPTER SIXTEEN

Last Call

"...Both Hollywood and the sport of body building have lost a true legend."

- Howard Mandell

New York Downtown Athletic Club, 2000

On May 1st, 2000, Steve Reeves died from complications due to a blood clot from surgery that previous morning. At seventy-four years old, the number one box-office star of *Hercules,* and world-renowned Mr. America, Mr. World and Mr. Universe was now gone. Just months prior, Steve had been diagnosed with lymphatic cancer and in turn began losing strength and body weight.

Looking back at the fall of 1999, I was speaking with Reeves on the phone several times a month upon the completion of my book *Worlds To Conquer*. Steve was grateful that he had just received in the mail a full case of them, something I said I would do upon its final press run. Overall, Reeves was very pleased with the much-anticipated biography. He very much liked how his story was presented, as well as the large, heavy stock presentation and chosen photos.

Unfortunately, since Steve's passing a few supporters of Reeves' are under the impression that Steve did not fully approve and authorize my final manuscript which is totally false, and inaccurate. There were only two details in the book that Reeves and I initially disputed over regarding my findings through research and interviews. The first being that Steve always thought that his parents had never separated or divorced when he was still an infant prior to his father's fatal farming accident. Steve's Uncle Clair, his mother's brother who I personally met and interviewed recalled in full detail his remembrance of his sisters failed marriage, as well as his fathers handed down family lore. The second misunderstanding was that Steve thought he competed and won the 1947 Mr. Western America, instead of the 1947 Mr. Pacific Coast Contest. I pointed out to Steve that he had two first-place trophies for the 1946 and 1947 Mr. Pacific Coast contests in his trophy case with his name engraved on them. I had also provided Steve with several supporting articles from each contest detailing the event and his wins. Reeves for whatever reason believed that he had never won any contest twice in a row, as he had with the Mr. Pacific Coast contests. After much discussion and debate, Steve finally agreed with me over both topics and gave the go ahead for printing. These were the only two issues Steve had with my entire manuscript. Reeves had praised me overall for my achievement and said once again, *"Chris, A lot of people over the years have promised to write a book about me, and you are the only one that made this happen. So, congratulations, you did a good job."*

So, for the record, Steve Reeves did fully authorize *Worlds To Conquer* prior to printing and release, regardless of what others choose to say or believe.

As for our continued phone calls, I would speak with Reeves throughout the winter of 1999 and 2000, discussing with him various book signings and promotions I had scheduled for *Worlds To Conquer* here on the East Coast. We would also briefly speak of various other topics as usual, such as current workout routines and diet, and of course the dating scene, and what ladies were now in my life. Steve always offered advice to me regarding women, which I was more than happy to receive especially from someone such as he who attracted tens of thousands of beautiful women throughout the world. But ironically, not once did Steve ever mention to me of his incurable illness. When I look back on these conversations, I truly believe pride was the primary reason why Steve never mentioned to me of his cancer. Both, the will to live and his dignity were now Steve's largest marquee's in life.

Upon learning of his death, I was also stunned to hear that Steve and Deborah had recently broken up just months prior to his passing on May 1st. Deborah had not only moved into the lower guest house on the property, but in addition with a new boyfriend. This new relationship of Deborah's quickly elevated to a legal marriage between her and her partner. Englehorn had stated her reasons of sudden and private matrimony while Steve was still alive in her 2014 self-published memoir *Steve Reeves: Legends Never Die*, *"...What started out on March 31, 2000, as a marriage of convenience so I could obtain health insurance and save my life, turned out to be the best relationship either Gene or I ever experienced..."* It is not known whether Steve ever knew of Deborah's private marriage prior to his passing, she did though occasionally assist Steve with various errands such as driving him to doctor appointments due to his increasing weakness and lack of stamina.

Even though Deborah and Steve exchanged private vows at a small Wyoming church the two visited back in 1994, the two were never officially married prior to their break-up. They were never married through the justice of the peace, nor through the conventional church or court system. As for common-law marriage the state of California does not recognize the statute among couples. So, for the record Steve Reeves was only legally married twice in his life, first to Sandra Smith in 1955, and lastly to Aline Czarjarwicz in 1963, and never to Deborah Englehorn.

On May 2nd, I received a phone call from the New York Downtown Athletic Club informing me that Reeves had succumbed to his cancer the day before. I was both shocked and saddened at the same time.

As his official biographer, I was immediately bombarded with telephone calls from all of the leading fitness magazines, as well as from nationwide newspapers asking for statements from me being Reeves official biographer regarding his passing.

I had also learned that Reeves' estate was now at the hands of the probate court due to the fact that Steve only had a *last will and testament*, rather than a *living trust*.

After eighteen-months held up in probate, the judge finally decided to grant Deborah as the primary awardee to Steve's entire savings as well as his fourteen-acre horse ranch. Even though Englehorn was never legally married to Steve, and was now married to Earl, Deborah was entitled to the majority of Steve's estate, with the understanding that all taxes, debts and administrative costs were first paid off. In addition, Reeves' will read that Deborah would receive a yearly annuity of fifty-thousand dollars for the rest of her life, as noted in Englehorn's memoir *Steve Reeves: Legends Never Die*.

It was not long after Steve's passing that Deborah sold the ranch and purchased a smaller home on the west side of Valley Center with her new husband Earl, until his passing in 2014.

The only actual Reeves Boyce family funeral service held for Steve was back in his home state of Montana, on his mother's side of the family with remaining relatives and friends. Several months later in 2000 I was invited to the event at the family Boyce cattle ranch in Lewistown where the outdoor service was held. The funeral organizer was Troy Bertelsen, a recent friend to Steve who ironically was the last person to visit and be with Reeves at his hospital-side bed the moment he passed away. Steve's uncle Clair Boyce also arranged the service bringing together various aunts, uncles and cousins of Steve's, as well as neighbors. Roughly thirty people were in attendance paying homage to Steve's amazing life and journey.

Atop a grassy hillside, undisturbed by flowing green fields and flowering meadows, just outside the small town of Lewistown Reeves' ashes were finally dispersed into the big sky and fertile lands of Montana where it all began for the proud, cowboy native.

Steve Reeves was now home.

Author Christopher LeClaire stands beside Steve Reeves' first bred Morgan horse *Monte*, a twenty-nine-year old stallion during Steve's funeral at his mother's family ranch in Lewistown, Montana, 2000. Troy Bertelsen photo

CHRONOLOGY

of Body Building Titles, Major Stage, Television Roles and Film

BODY BUILDING TITLES

1946 Mr. Pacific Coast, Portland, Oregon. December 21st.; Steve Reeves (1st. place), Don Malucci (2nd.), Mario Gregor (3rd.).

1947 Mr. Pacific Coast, Los Angles, California. Embassey Auditorium. May 24th.; Steve Reeves (1st. place, and awarded "Best Arms," "Best Chest," "Best Legs"), Eric Pedersen (2nd.), Bill Cantrell (3rd.).

1947 Mr. America, Chicago, Illinois. Lane Tech. Auditorium. June 29th.; Steve Reeves (1st. place, and awarded "Best Back"), Eric Pedersen (2nd.), Joe Lauriano (3rd).

1948 Mr. USA, Los Angeles, California. Shrine Auditorium. March 15th.; Clarence Ross (1st. place), Steve Reeves (2nd.), Alan Stephan (3rd.).

1948 Mr. Universe, London, England. Padallium Auditorium. August 13th.; John Grimek (1st. place), Steve Reeves (2nd.), Andre Drapp (3rd.).

1948 Mr. World, Cannes, France. Cannes Holiday Resort. August 16th.; Steve Reeves (1st. place, also awarded 'Le Plus Bel Athlete' award), Sylvestre Lindberg (2nd.), Robert Duranton (3rd.).

1949, Mr USA, Los Angeles, California. Shrine Auditorium. March 26th.; John Grimek (**I** st. place), Clarence Ross (2nd.), Steve Reeves (3rd.).

1950 Mr. Universe, London, England. Scala Theatre. June 24th.; Steve Reeves (1st. place), Reg Park (2nd.), Hubert Thomas (3rd.).

STAGE

Kismet, 1953-55, national road company tour, starring Alfred Drake. Steve Reeves first Broadway appearance. Steve played a Wazir guard.

Wish You Were Here, 1955, starring Beverly Bozeman, in summer stock production in Sacramento, California. Steve played Muscles, the fifth lead. A Milton Lyon production.

The Vamp, 1955, starring Carol Channing. Reeves last Broadway performance. He played two leads: Samson, and Muscle Man.

TELEVISION

The Ralph Edwards Show, (NBC) ran for one season, premiering September 1 st., 1955, and ending September,1952.

Kimbar, Lord Of The Jungle, (CBS) half-hour pilot, filmed November, 1952. The intended mini-series was never purchased for release.

Steve also made guest appearances on *The Red Skeleton Show, The Ozzie & Harriet Show, Topper, The Burns & Allen Show,* and *The Dinah Shore Show.*

FILMS

Jail Bait

(1954, US) Howco Productions 80 mins. B/W; DIR: Edward D. Wood, Jr.. PROD: Edward D. Wood, Jr.. SCR: Alex Gordon, Edward D. Wood, Jr.. PH: William Thompson. MUS: Hoyt Kurtain. With Lyle Talbot, Delores Fuller, Vic Brady. Steve Reeves (as "Lt. Bob Lawrence").

Athena

(1954, US) Metro-Goldwyn-Mayer 96 min. Color; DIR: Richard Thorpe. With Debbie Reynolds, Jane Powell, Edmund Purdom, Vic Damone. Steve Reeves (as "Ed Perkins").

Hercules

(1957, Italy) Galatea-Oscar Films 105 min. Color; DIR: Pietro Fracisci. PROD: Federico Teti. SCR: Pietro Fracisci, Ennio DeConcini, Gaio Frattini. PH: Mario Bava. MUS: Enzo Masetti.

With Steve Reeves (as "Hercules"), Sylva Koscina, Mimmo Palmara, Giana Maria Canale.

Hercules Unchained

(1958, Italy) Lux-Galatea Film 105 min. Color; DIR: Pietro Fracisci. PROD: Bruno Vailati. SCR: Pietro Fracisci, Ennio DeConcini. PH: Mario Bava. MUS: Enzo Masetti. With Steve Reeves (as "Hercules"), Sylva Koscina, Sylvia Lopez,

Mimmo Palmera, Primo Camera.

The White Warrior

(1959, Italy) Majestic Films 110 min. Color; DIR: Riccardo Freda. PROD: Tommaso Sagone. SCR: Luigi DeSanctis, Akos Tolnay, (based on a short story by Leo Tolstoy). PH: Leopoldo Savona. With Steve Reeves (as "Hadji Murad"), Georgia Moll, Scilla Gabel.

Goliath And The Barbarians

(1959, Italy) Standard Productions 95 min. Color; DIR: Carlo Campogalliani. PROD: Emmimo Salvi. SCR: Emmimo Salvi, Gino Mangini. PH: Adalberto Albertini. MUS: Carlo Inncenti. With Steve Reeves (as "Emilio"), Chelo Alonso, Bruce Cabot.

The Last Days Of Pompeii

(1959, Italy) Cine Productions 103 min. Color; DIR: Mario Bonnard. PROD: Paolo Moffa . SCR: Ennino DeConcini, Sergio Leone, Sergio Corbucci, Duccio Tessari. PH: Antonio Lopez Ballesteros. MUS: Angelo Francesco Lavagnino. With Steve Reeves (as "Glaucus"), Christine Kauffmann, Mimmo Palmara, Anne Marie Baumann.

The Giant Of Marathon

(1960, Italy) Titanus-Galatea Films 105 min. Color; DIR: Jacques Tourneur. PROD: Bruno Vailati. PH: Mario Bava. MUS: Roberto Nicolosi. With Steve Reeves (as "Phillipides"), Mylene Demongeot, Daniela Rocca.

Morgan The Pirate

(1960, Italy) Adelphia 93 min. Color; DIR: Andre De Toth. PROD: Lux-Adelphia Prods. SCR: Primo Zeglio, Andre De Toth, Filipo Sanjust. PH: Tonino Delli Colli. MUS: Franco Mannino. With Steve Reeves (as "Henry Morgan"), Valerie Lagrange, Chelo Alonso.

The Thief Of Baghdad

(1961, Italy) Lux-Titanus 89 min. Color; DIR: Arthur Lubin. PROD: Bruno Vailati. SCR: Augusto Frassinetti, Filippo Sanjust, Bruno Vailati. PH: Tonino Delli Colli. MUS: Carlo Rustichelli. With Steve Reeves (as "Karim"), Georgia Moll, Arturo Dominici.

The Trojan Horse

(1961, Italy) Borderie Films 95 min. Color; DIR: Giorgio Ferroni. PROD: Gianpaolo Bigazzi. SCR: Ugo Liberatone. PH: Rino Filippini. With Steve Reeves (as "Aeneas"), John Drew Barrymore, Jr., Juliette Mayniel, Hedy Vessel.

Duel Of The Titans

(1961, Italy) Titanus Films 96 min. Color; DIR: Sergio Corbucci. PROD: Franco Palaggi. SCR: Luciano Martino, Sergio Leone, Sergio Corbucci. PH: Franco Giraldi. With Steve Reeves (as "Romulos"), Virna Lisi, Gordon Scott.

The Avenger (The Legend Of Aeneas)

(1962, Italy) Mercury Films 102 min. B/W; DIR: Albert Band. PROD: Albert Band, Giorgio Venturini. SCR: Ugo Liberatore, Arrigo Montanari, Luigi Mangini, Nino Stresa. PH: Angelo Lotti. MUS: Giovanni Fusco. With Steve Reeves (as "Aeneas"), Carla Marlier, Liana Orfei, Giana Garko.

The Slave (The Son Of Spartacus)

(1962, Italy) Titanus Films 95 min. Color; DIR: Sergio Corbucci. PROD: Franco Giraldi. SCR: Adriano Bolzoni. PH: Enzo Barboni. MUS: Piero Piccioni. With Steve Reeves (as "Rando"), Gianna Maria Canale, Jacques Sernas.

Sandokan The Great

(1963, Italy) Centra Films 114 min. Color; DIR: Umberto Lenzi. PROD: Robert DeNesle. SCR: Fulvio Gicca, Umberto Lenzi, (based on Emilio Salgari's novel "The Tiger of Mompracem). PH: Angelo Lotti, Giovanni Scarpellini. MUS: Giovanni Fusca. With Steve Reeves (as "Sandokan"), Genevieve Grad, Andre Bosic.

Sandokan (Pirates Of The Seven Seas)

(1963, Italy) Filmes 107 min. Color; DIR: Umberto Lenzi. PROD: Solly V. Bianco. SCR: Umberto Lenzi, (based on Emilio Salgari's novel "Pirates Of Malaya"). PH: Angelo Loti. MUS: Giovanni Fusco. With Steve Reeves (as "Sandokan"), Jacqueline Sassard, Mimmo Palmara.

A Long Ride From Hell

(1968, Italy) B.R.C. Films 104 min. Color; DIR: Alex Burks. PROD: Roberto Natale, Steve Reeves. SCR: Roberto Natale, Steve Reeves, (based on Gordon Shirreffs novel "Judas Gun"). PH: Enzo Barboni. MUS: Carlo Savina. With Steve Reeves (as "Mike Stages"), Wayde Preston, Mimmo Palmera, Silvana Ventaelli.

*

Steve is said to have also appeared as an extra in ***Conquest of Mycene*** aka ***Hercules Attacks)*** (1963) starring Gordon Scott.

A film crew captures a romantic moment with Sylva Koscina and Steve Reeves in *Hercules*, 1957. Courtesy Steve Reeves

ACKNOWLEDGEMENTS

First and foremost, I thank God for his guidance, love, and protection and the grateful gifts of mind, body, and spirit. I thank my family, Col. Hillary LeClaire and my sister Hope for their love and support, and my mother Anne. I thank her especially for assisting with the manuscript, between all of the countless edits and tiring rewrites we were still able to find laughter and enjoyment along the way.

I want to thank Steve Reeves for this great opportunity, to write his incredible life story, and the trust, time and teachings he provided me with during this seven-year journey of mine at writing his life story. I also thank Reeves for providing me with the majority of the photos for *Worlds To Conquer*. I wish you all the best Steve, take care!

I thank the following organizations and staffs who provided generous aid and assistance as well; The Library of Congress, The New York Public Theatre Library, The Oakland Public Library, The Cape Cod Community College Library, The Daniels County Museum, Santa Monica International Gymnastic Hall of Fame and New York's Downtown Athletic Club.

Special thanks also to the two amazing publishers and promoters within the sport of bodybuilding; Joe Weider of *Muscle & Fitness* magazine, and Robert Kennedy of *Muscle Mag International* magazine. I thank you both for your generous lending of photographs, and back issues of your magazines for reproduction in this book. In addition, I thank you for the complementary advertising and book reviews you provided for *Worlds To Conquer*. I also thank body building historian Joe Roark for his assistance in sharing his abundant knowledge within the sport.

I thank the following who took so many of the incredible photos of Steve throughout his lifetime, as well as his family and friends that lent them to me for this book; Claire and Edna Boyce, Russ Warner, Tony Lanza, Gregor Arax, Paul-Stone Raymor, Constantine, George Greenwood, Goldie Reeves, Anthony Norvell, Ed and Alyce Yarick, John Terpak, Herb Ball, and Will Raport to name but a few.

I also thank the following collectors who provided additional source material, photographs, and memorabilia; Joe Sciambra, Milton T. Moore, Jr., George Coates, Giuseppe Alletto, Pierre Charles, and Bill Hinbern.

Lastly, I thank the following people for their additional assistance with this biography; Rodman Miller, Lavina Powell, Edgar Richardson, Larry Bowler, Gloria and Ray Hartman, Clancy Ross, Bob and Elise Weidlich, Troy Bertelsen, Frank Zane, Joe Corsi, George Eiferman, Carol Channing, Bruce Lundy, Rudy Riska, Deborah Englehorn, Jack and Elaine LaLanne.

About the Author

Christopher LeClaire is a former U.S. Navy DIVER and served during Operation Desert Storm. He graduated with honors from *The University of Massachusetts Dartmouth* earning a BFA *cum laude*. He recently graduated from The Massachusetts Police Academy MPTC and is currently a Reserve Deputy Sheriff with the County Sheriff's Office. He resides on Cape Cod.

Printed in Dunstable, United Kingdom

71547082R00163